Holly Jolly Holidays

By

Gayle Carline

Cover art by Joe Felipe of Market Me
(www.marketme.us).

ISBN: 1-943654-04-2
ISBN-13: 978-1-943654-04-8

Published in USA by Dancing Corgi Press

DEDICATION

To Placentia, and all its lovely people

ACKNOWLEDGMENTS

Thank you to Heather McRae and the Placentia News-Times for publishing my weekly musings.

Thank you to my husband Dale and our son Marcus for letting me talk about them in my weekly musings.

Thank you to the schools and organizations of Placentia, from Valencia High School, to the Placentia Library, to the Rotary and Women's clubs, for including me and my family. We value our time with you.

And most of all, thank you to the citizens of Placentia who read my musings and tell me how much they love them—or even how much they hate them.

I love you all.

CONTENTS

It's Not Just Christmas, You Know

In 2005, I began writing a weekly humor column for the Placentia News-Times, the local paper that is affiliated with the Orange County Register. My columns are a slice-of-life look at an average woman who is a wife, mother, homeowner, and city resident—in other words, me.

When I thought of a holiday-centered book, I intended to include of my holiday columns, from New Year's musings, Mother's Day fantasies, all the way to the inevitable Christmas.

Then I counted how many I had written in 10 years. There were over 80 essays. That's a lot of jolly holidays. In reading these columns, I've noticed two common themes: gratitude and hope, both of which I possess in abundance

I'm grateful for the opportunity to write for the paper, as well as for the feedback I get from readers. And I hope these essays resonate with you as much as they have my Placentia friends.

THANKSGIVING

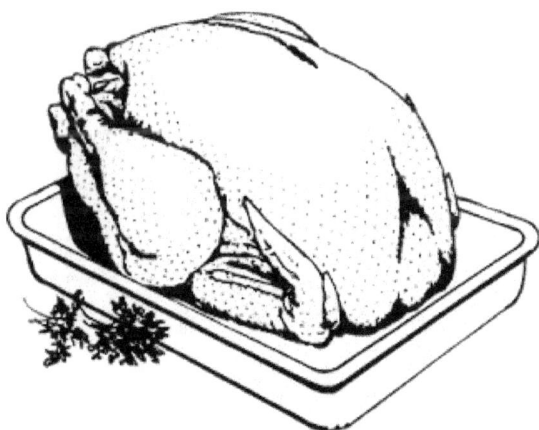

GIVING THANKS FOR THE LITTLE THINGS

Thanksgiving is here, swimming in traditions as rich as the cornbread stuffing and gravy. Most of us will gather with our extended families, lay our diets aside for a day and give thanks for all of the important things in our lives.

We are thankful for our health and our loved ones, the roof over our heads and the meal on the table. Some of us will remember to be thankful for living in freedom, and will pause to reflect on the less fortunate.

But what about the Thanksgiving "B" list, the little things that may not seem essential, but save our sanities? Just for the holiday, I've jotted down a few of the smaller items for which I'm truly grateful.

For example, I'm thankful that my son, Marcus, plays his video games in his room now. Their music has begun to drive me batty, especially when Marcus plays them in the family room and I fall asleep on the couch. I have very disturbing dreams after hearing the same four bars of "The Legend of Zelda" repeating for more than a half hour.

I'm thankful that my husband, Dale, knows how to cook. I'm also grateful that he doesn't do it too often because he's not really into cleaning up afterward. His cooking style is very Southern, so practically everything starts with a roux and ends with something being fried. It all tastes great, but I'm the one chipping the cemented flour and oil off of the stove in the morning.

I'm thankful that Dale's cell phone is the worst thing I've ruined in the laundry. My mother actually dried our cat in the dryer once. Don't worry, she discovered him after just a couple of spins. He survived, but he was a little dizzy for a few days.

I'm really thankful that the Turner Classic Movies channel still does not consider "RoboCop" to be a timeless masterpiece. If I'm lucky, I'll age to the point where today's films will be shown on classic movie channels, but for now, I can still have Tracy and Hepburn, Bogie and Bacall, and even Abbott and Costello.

Speaking of television, I'm thankful that my life is not a reality show. The problem with having your life under a microscope to be scrutinized by millions of viewers is that those viewers think they're entitled to an opinion about what they see in the lens. I'm not interested in what millions of strangers think about me after watching an hour of TV that has been culled from my daily life.

I have many more things on my B-list, from being thankful for Marcus' improving hygiene (why are boys so allergic to soap?) to having a Cheesecake Factory in Brea. These things may not be important, but I'm glad I have them.

So when the turkey is passed around, I will be thankful for all of the true blessings in my life. By the time the pumpkin pie is cut, I'll be giving thanks for the little things... like whipped cream.

THANKFUL FOR THE STRESS

Of all the holidays, Thanksgiving stresses me out the most. It's not the cooking or entertaining that makes me nervous, or even spending the day trapped in a house with quirky relatives. It's because I never know what we are doing until the week before the event. I know I'll be eating turkey somewhere, I just don't know where. I suppose I should just relax and be thankful, but sometimes I can't see the flock for all of the birds.

When I was young, Thanksgiving was always hosted at my grandparents' house. Grandma spent a week cooking so we could invade her home like locusts, fight over who sat where, and eat until our stomachs hurt. And as soon as the pain lessened, we'd eat some more. For years, my Thanksgiving was planned and life was good.

Now that I'm an adult with my own family,

Thanksgiving has become more ambiguous. My grandparents passed away long ago, and my family is two thousand miles from us, so that tradition is out of our reach. Dale's family does not have a big Thanksgiving meal; everyone is scattered and Dale's mom usually spends most of the day in church.

One year we tried to gather everyone together for Thanksgiving, but something got lost in the translation and they all showed up two hours late. It was quite a battle for me to keep everything warm while we waited. At one point, I walked into the kitchen to find our cat straddling the turkey and gnawing on the breast.

After that, we decided to find something else to do.

For several years now, we have teamed up with our friends, the Derbys, who are also alone on Thanksgiving, switching houses every year. This works pretty well, except that we usually can't remember who hosted dinner last year, and no one calls anyone until the last minute.

This year, I have the added problem of my plumbing fiasco cleanup. Until I get my new flooring in the bedroom, there are shoes and bags and boxes in the living room. It's not a décor that I want to show off to company, so it's hard to feel relaxed or thankful.

I found an article on the Internet about how to have a stress-free Thanksgiving. It was written by Martha Stewart, who certainly should know something about stress. There were some really good ideas—for women who are just like Martha. I'm not sure about the rest of us.

For example, four days before Thanksgiving, she suggests putting the frozen turkey in the refrigerator to thaw slowly. Sounds good, but she left out the step where I have to remove all of the leftovers that are now science experiments in order to fit the turkey into the fridge.

9

She also recommends making the pie crusts on that fourth day and freezing them. Hasn't that woman ever heard of Marie Callender's?

Two days before the event, Martha wants to get out the china and flatware, and iron the napkins. I tried that once, but the paper sticks to the iron.

She even has a Thanksgiving Day schedule to get you from kitchen to table in eight hours. Unfortunately, it doesn't have an entry for airing out the house when you've burned the gravy, or running to the store because your son ate all of the olives.

I guess I should just relax and enjoy the holiday. After all, I know I will be eating turkey somewhere, whether it's just with Dale and Marcus, or with an extended group of friends. And even if I am stressed, I can still find something to be thankful for, especially Marie's pies.

SOMETIMES GRATITUDE IS FOR THE IMMEDIATE THINGS

Usually, I spend Thanksgiving being thankful I am not Martha Stewart's daughter, since I'm certain Martha would not sit down at a table with canned cranberry sauce wiggling in a bowl. But this year, there's so much more to earn my gratitude.

First of all, I'm thankful to live in a neighborhood that does not back up to miles of untamed wilderness. I understand the views are beautiful, but they come with a high price during times of severe drought and high winds. Even so, during the fires, I sat glued to my TV and the Internet, checking maps and wondering what would stop the fire from burning west to Placentia. The embers seemed to hopscotch from dried brush to eaves as they ate everything in their path. Thank God the firefighters did their jobs so well.

I am also thankful that, at least in the Triangle Complex fire, no lives were lost. Property loss is devastating, especially as the days pass and you start to remember what you no longer have, from photos to baby shoes. Life, however, is so much more valuable.

Grandma's china may be gone, but sharing turkey with loved ones is better, even if it's on paper plates.

My horses in Chino Hills escaped harm, too, for which I am grateful. I left the ranch on Saturday knowing that both the 57 and 91 freeways were already closed, so I took a chance on Carbon Canyon Road. It was the most surreal drive of my life. As I drove to the top of a hill, I saw bright blue skies behind me and a wall of black smoke in front of me. It is a natural instinct to move away from the smoke, toward the blue, and yet I was going in the opposite direction.

By the time I reached the entrance to Chino Hills State Park, I looked to my right and saw flames on the ridge behind a housing development.

I spent Sunday tracking the fire's progress down the canyon and into Chino Hills, feeling helpless. If my horses had to be evacuated, I would have no way to get over there to pitch in. I would have to trust my friend and trainer, to get my horses to safety.

Thankfully, I do trust her.

As intent as I was in monitoring the fire, my Yorba Linda friends were even more so, since they had to leave their homes. Some of them had a few minutes to figure out what they needed to take, some had mere moments, and a few of them weren't home when the evacuation orders came down, so they were caught without even a toothbrush. I am eternally grateful that their homes were spared, as well as their lives.

Believe it or not, I'm also thankful that Valencia High

School was designated as an evacuation center. We live a few blocks from the school, so it meant that, if VHS was a safe haven, our house was probably out of the fire zone, too. It felt nice to have Placentia serve as a place to shelter people in need.

Speaking of VHS, the only loss we suffered in the area had nothing to do with the fire. Our choir was holding a car wash at Del Taco when the strong winds discovered our EZ-Up canopy. Bricks and people couldn't hold it down. It flew into a few cars before splitting in two and coming to a clumping halt. Now we get to raise more funds for another canopy, so we can hold more fundraisers.

This year, I'm even thankful for that.

Holidays Need a Plan

It's Thanksgiving already, and I can't quite believe it. Didn't we just celebrate Independence Day?

I should have suspected The Holiday Season was just around the corner. Many stores had their Christmas decorations out in October, displayed next to the Halloween costumes in a strange kind of holiday fusion. But I've learned to ignore all displays for holidays that are over a month away.

It's not fair to make me stress over Christmas while I'm buying candy for the trick-or-treaters.

Strangely, this year I didn't notice any Thanksgiving advertising, either before or after October 31st, until last week. Suddenly, the newspapers were full of coupons for green beans and cream of mushroom soup. Albertson's was offering two turkeys for the price of one. Autumn leaves and pumpkins were everywhere I looked.

At least I only had one week to panic.

Most of my panic is the result of our family's tradition; for years, we didn't have one. My immediate family lives in Illinois, and even though Dale's family is local, I've developed a theory about Thanksgiving. I think people tend to spend it with the wife's family. Dale has one brother in Oregon and two brothers nearby. All of my sisters-in-law have close family in the area, so the chances of getting his entire family together are pretty slim. For one thing, we'd have to rent, like, the Coliseum to hold us all.

Our tradition for the past several years is to spend the day with our friends. The problem is that Sylvia and I forget until the last minute, when one of us calls the other, and no one can remember who hosted it last year.

If we decide dinner's at my house, I have to go into "list" mode. Clean the house, check. Make a list of groceries, check. Go to the store with the list, check. Clean the house again because the dog and cat have tossed hair all over the carpet, check. Go back to the store because I forgot to put something on the list, check.

By contrast, dinner at our friends' house requires only two things: sweet potato casserole and pumpkin pie. Throw in a bottle of wine and maybe some flowers for the hostess, and it's still a shorter list.

My dishes are nothing special. I found the sweet potato recipe online, after searching for some compromise between my desire to eat creamy, whipped sweet potatoes with plenty of marshmallows on top, and Dale's desire to leave sweet potatoes in a more pristine, non-whipped state. At least we agree on the marshmallows.

The pumpkin pie is even more basic - I use the recipe on the can of pumpkin. I don't even make my own pie crust. I have a little Doughboy in the refrigerator aisle for that. Sylvia told me once how much her son loves my pie, and I tried to explain that I am such a fraud, I just follow directions on pre-processed ingredients.

"Oh, no, you must do something different," she said. "I've followed those directions, too, and he doesn't like mine."

I suspect it has more to do with a teenager's desire to push their parents' buttons, which I'm pretty sure is a physical law, like gravity. Someday I'm going to test this theory, by making a pie and telling him his mom did it. We'll see how well he likes it then.

Having a plan is great, but I know Thanksgiving will come, whether we are with family, friends, or just each other. As long as I have a list, I'll be ready for it.

TAKING TIME FOR THANKS

Wow, is it Thanksgiving already? Wasn't it just summer? Actually, in southern California, you could point to sunshine and high temperatures about 300 days a year, and say, "Look, it's summer."

But the calendar says November is almost over, so I'd better think of what I'm thankful for this year. I'm always thankful for my health, a roof over my head, and family and friends. I hate repeating myself every Turkey Day, though, so I like to consider new things to appreciate.

This year, I'm thankful I don't have a dozen kids and am not a reality TV star. Even though I love being a writer and wouldn't mind having my book in every home in America, I don't want to be so famous that every move I make is scrutinized by the public. I get enough of that from my son.

Dale and I had planned on having two children, but

God pointed at me and said, "I really think you can only handle one." He was probably right, although Marcus made my job very easy. When I see the kinds of mischief other kids are causing, I feel completely blessed that my darkest hour with my son was when I realized he'd never keep his room clean.

Let me apologize to his future spouse (whoever she might be) right now: I tried, Dear, but he was born with the clutter gene.

I'm also thankful I've never wanted to run for public office. I admire the people who see something wrong with their neighborhood and want to fix it instead of complain about it. And I've often said, my perfect job would be to sit in a comfy chair and give people my opinion all day, which is how I'd describe most political candidates. However, I don't think I could muster the nerve to sell my opinions as being the will of the people.

I know from experience, people don't always vote for you because they agree with your agenda. Back in the old days, my high school held a ceremony on the Sunday before graduation. Awards were presented and a local pastor gave an encouraging speech. We got to vote for the pastor. There were four or five names, but I remember who we selected, and I remember why.

His name was Dr. Frankenstein. I hope you're not waiting for me to explain.

I think it's going to be a cold shock to a lot of newly elected officials to find out no one wants to implement their ideas, they just liked their smile or thought they had a cool name or voted the party line.

Lastly, I'm thankful my husband is my complete opposite, in almost every way. Sure, we're both adventurous in our tastes, from trying new food to trying new music. But where I want to talk about everything, during every waking hour, he sums up his day with a quiet shrug. When I want to call the plumber at four in the morning to fix the leak, he wants to evaluate the damage and see if he can fix it. While I try to teach the puppy discipline, he wrestles him into a frenzy.

Each of these things could mean doom for a relationship, but I'm happy. I know they mean I get all the talking time because he doesn't want any, we ultimately save money by not fixing things right away, and the puppy can tell the difference between Mommy and The Fun Guy.

I have a lot to be thankful for, and I hope you do, too.

GRATEFUL FOR LIFE'S LEMONS

Today is Thanksgiving, a day we think about the blessings in our lives and show our gratitude by gathering together with family and friends. We begin with a large meal, followed by naps and football games.

It's an exhausting celebration.

This year, I'm focused on the things in my life that most people would not see as positive. Lately, I've been watching all the celebrities in the news. I don't want to watch them, but they are difficult to ignore. As usual, they are doing things that are not particularly healthy or smart. And, as usual, there are plenty of gossip columnists and photographers to record their deeds.

I realize how thankful I am not to be one of these famous people. I feel sorry for them, not because they are hounded by the media constantly. If you want to be famous, I figure paparazzi go with the territory.

I feel sorry because they don't know any better than to do stupid things. It seems they have been raised in such a cocoon of wealth, they have been protected from the kind of life that teaches everyone else common sense.

Get caught with drugs? They have enough money to hire an attorney who will keep them out of jail. Have second thoughts about marriage? Again, there is enough money for both parties to turn around and keep walking. In their world, there is almost no problem that can't be solved by throwing money at it. In fact, the only problem they can't seem to solve is how to learn from their mistakes.

My parents weren't poverty-level poor, but my dad worked three jobs to make the $80-a-month house payment and put food on the table. Dale's family circumstances were similar. We didn't starve, but each dollar was stretched as far as it could go.

When I moved out of my parents' house, I had thrift-store furniture in my apartment, and ate peanut butter and crackers to save money when the rent was due. I still managed to do stupid things, but I knew Mom and Dad couldn't be there with a checkbook to bail me out.

They were only going to show up to give me their opinion of my choices.

When children of affluent families get into trouble, I often hear people say, "They have everything. How can they be so ungrateful?"

I used to think that, until recently, when it dawned upon me: they can't be ungrateful. They would have to know what poverty feels like in order to be thankful for what they have. Money doesn't guarantee a happy family, but they at least feel financially secure, because they have never known any other life.

Not only do I now feel more empathetic toward these people, I am also more thankful for my own upbringing. I appreciate being taught to live within my means. I'm glad for those endless nights of canned tuna and noodles for dinner. I feel blessed for the times of searching through the sofa for loose change to pay the electric bill.

I'm especially happy that some of my worst ideas were squelched because I knew I couldn't afford an attorney, but my parents' wrath was free.

So this Thanksgiving I shall sit in front of a nice, big plate of turkey and dressing, and think about all the times my plate wasn't so full. I will say a prayer for those who still go hungry, and I'll say one for those who don't understand their own good fortune.

This year, I will be grateful that life has taught me gratitude.

THANKFUL FOR THE BIG THINGS, TOO

Author's note: This particular column was written after I had taken a brief hiatus from the newspaper. I ran for Placentia Library District Trustee, and voting laws say my opponents would have the right to the same publicity generated by my weekly column.

I'm so glad to be back, I barely know where to start. It seems like a lot of has changed, but Dale is still at Raytheon, Marcus is still at college, and I'm still juggling writing with housework, two dogs, two horses, and a cat.

Maybe not that much has changed after all.

I couldn't think of a better time to return than Thanksgiving. I am thankful for many things. First, I'm always thankful for my family. Dale is supportive of my writing career and I support his Fantasy Football, even if I don't understand it. Marcus is making fabulous music at Cal

State Long Beach and now that he's in an apartment, I don't have to nag him about cleaning his room.

I'm also thankful to be able to work in any capacity at the Placentia Library, but doubly thankful to be a trustee. I'm grateful to the citizens of Placentia for electing me. I'll do my best to make you proud.

Next, I'm thankful to have met so many of my readers at the various events this summer, and the Heritage Day celebration. Lots of you wanted to know where my column went and told me how much you like knowing that someone out there goes through the same things you do.

I missed you, too.

Lately, I'm thankful for good health insurance. I'm writing this column two days before I undergo cataract surgery on my right eye. I've been seeing the world through an increasingly thick layer of fog for almost a year. The bad part is that I get disoriented easily in low light, and nighttime driving is frightening. The good part is that when I need to avoid someone, I just blame it on the cataract.

I'll need a new excuse now that I'll be able to see again.

Cataract surgery is very quick and easy these days. They tell you that you can drive the next day. They also tell you that the following actions are forbidden for up to two weeks: lifting heavy objects, bending over, rubbing your eye, getting water or dust in it, or wearing makeup.

For an easy surgery with a fast recovery, there are a lot of rules.

The part about lifting heavy objects and bending over interfered with Thanksgiving this year. We usually alternate with another family, and this was our year to host. Suddenly, not only could I not lift the turkey, I couldn't even lean over to baste it. Dale offered to help. He's a great cook, but I started thinking about all of the pre-dinner housecleaning and shopping that I couldn't do. Marcus is still busy with classes, so I did the only think I could think of.

I panicked.

Calling my friend, I threw myself on her mercy and asked if we could switch years and come to their house this year instead. Sylvia is the nicest, most delightful of friends, and agreed immediately. I even offered to bring my tiara for her to wear all day. She deserves it.

So this year, in addition to being thankful for my family, for my health, and for being able to do what I love, I am eternally thankful for the chance to sit around a table and share a meal with good friends.

Bring on the pumpkin pie.

WEEPING WITH GRATITUDE

It's Thanksgiving week, and I could be writing about all the bustle of the day and perhaps tell a funny story about a cooking disaster. When it comes to cooking, I have plenty of funny stories—and disasters.

Instead, though, I'd rather talk about gratitude.

Lately, I've been experiencing odd feelings of sentimentality. I admit, I've always misted up at Hallmark commercials and there are movies that can make me cry every time I watch them.

Darn you, Bambi.

As I grow older, I find myself choking up and feeling thankful for everything, from my morning coffee to a stranger's smile. To be fair, many folks are thankful that I've had my morning coffee.

I suspect part of the reason is because Marcus turned

21, making me the mother of an adult. I'm not constantly thinking about his childhood, or reliving the past. But subconsciously, I must be aware that he's all grown up and my job as a mom needs to move into an advisory role.

It's uncharted territory for a woman who likes to make things happen.

The other day, my horse trainer Niki told me about something cute her two-year-old did and I felt myself making that "aww" face, complete with shiny eyes. I wasn't thinking of my own son when she was telling me about Tyler, but there was a feeling that I had experienced the same thing when Marcus was that age.

All she would have had to do was show me a picture of him and I would have wept.

To add to my emotional roller coaster, Dale is retiring. Yes, it's early retirement. No, he's not that old. He can't be that old, because I'm older than he is, and I'm still youthful.

Aren't I?

When I tell people that my husband is retiring, some of them get a pensive look to their faces and ask how I feel about it. On and off the record, let me assure everyone that I'm not worried. Dale is a guy with both hobbies and projects. He has his own list of things to do. I may have a few suggestions of my own.

The bottom line is he's not a man who enjoys boredom.

Marcus may be more concerned than any of us. I was discussing his college expenses recently, trying to reassure him that we had plenty of money.

"Don't worry, you'll be a millionaire when we go," I said.

"You're okay, though, right?" he asked.

"Yes, we just had physicals. We're both super healthy."

"Good," he told me. "Because I'm tearing up here just thinking about it."

So this Thanksgiving, I have much to be thankful for. I enjoy good health. I even enjoy the muscle aches of working too hard, since there are people who are physically incapable of lifting a saddle or pushing a broom.

My family is a constant source of peace and delight. Dale is the calm in any storm we might face, the man who will stand at the center of a hurricane and say, "Now, wait, let's think about this." Marcus has been, and continues to be a joy to me, as a person as well as a son. We have a roof over our heads and food in our pantry, and have time to relax as well as work.

Mostly, I'm thankful that I don't have to wait until Thanksgiving to show my gratitude. We can all do that every day.

RACING THROUGH THE HOLIDAYS REQUIRES STAMINA

When Dale and I went to Scotland in September, I was a little shocked by the hotels, already offering deals on Christmas parties and lodging. Then I came home and saw cardboard Santas pointing at the Halloween candy.

From September through December, our celebrations seem to run together in one mad dash toward the New Year. I guess the good news is that at least in the states, we don't celebrate Hogmanay, a spectacular Scottish tradition of ringing in January 1st with presents, music, dance, and lighting things on fire, including replica Viking ships.

Even in January, I'm not about to set fire to anything. It's bad for southern California.

Now that Halloween has been put to bed, it's time to get out those construction-paper turkeys and prepare for

Thanksgiving. Dale and I share the day with our friends, the Derbys. We try to alternate hosting duties, although our friends have probably hosted more than we have.

This is our year, which means I should have started cleaning the house in July.

When you combine two dogs, one cat, and a writer trying to finish a novel, you get a messy home. I walk through every morning, see the dust, and think, "Gee, someone should take care of that."

Then I go try to extract 2,000 words out of my head and onto the page.

In addition to cleaning, there's some straightening and organizing to do. Things have a way of leaving their closets and cabinets, and tossing themselves on couches and tables. At least, I think they do it themselves—no one else in the house ever confesses to leaving a mess.

We have a four-bedroom house, which means we have two spare rooms. One is called "the computer room" because that's where computers go to die in our house. The room is currently awash in unfiled papers and horse show equipment, and I have vowed to clean it before the Derbys come over.

My horse trainer asked, "Does your company have to see that room?"

"No, they never look in it," I told her. Then my eyes narrowed and I whispered, "But I'll know where the mess is."

This is also the first year we've hosted with two dogs underfoot. Duffy was pretty easy to disregard, but the Lady Spazzleton has enough heft to make her presence known. I try not to subject guests to my canine horde, unless they are truly dog people, so the puppies will spend the day in the yard, wearing bark collars and looking sad.

Don't worry, they'll have plenty of treats when the party's over.

While I vacuum, I'll be thinking about the grocery list. My first task will be to find a turkey that's big enough without approaching ostrich-size. Then I have to get ingredients for side dishes and desserts. I've been ignoring all the grocery displays of pumpkin filling and cranberry sauce until now, so I'll chuck a few of those in my cart. Of course, what I'd really like is a recipe using Halloween candy in the Thanksgiving meal.

How do you think M&Ms would taste in the stuffing?

Two weeks from now, it will all be over and we'll be waking from our turkey extravaganza to plan Christmas. I'll have just enough energy for a safe and sane New Year's Eve. Too bad I can't burn a Viking ship.

CHRISTMAS

GAYLE CARLINE

SNAPPING THE CHRISTMAS PHOTO

After awakening from our turkey-induced coma, my family did what it does every Thanksgiving weekend: we took our Christmas picture. This event gets more out of control every year, and it's pretty much my fault.

When Marcus was a baby, we dressed up, went to the Brea Mall and sat in front of a mural of a Christmas tree. It was all very civil and we had nice pictures to include in all of our cards. By the time he was three, we abandoned the idea of planning ahead, and sat in front of our own fireplace, fiddling with the camera's timer until we used up all the film.

As our various pets arrived, I decided it would be cute to include them. From Marcus' point of view, it was necessary, since we had stockings for each one (yes, even the gecko). So our cat, Katy, and dog, Mikey, began appearing in the photos. We gave up on the gecko after one session, when we discovered that cats and dogs think geckos are toys.

Despite my attempt to prepare for this event, every year, I'd get out my camera to discover that there were only six shots left and no other film in the house. So we'd try to get the most mileage out of six pictures, taken with a cat who was squirming to escape and a dog who was interested in what the cat was doing. Never mind the three people who were closing their eyes, opening their mouths, or making weird faces.

Then I bought my horse, Frostie, and decided that she needed to be in the picture, too. We couldn't bring 900 pounds home to stand next to the fireplace. So, as Dr. Seuss said, I "had a wonderful, awful idea." Why not take the rest of the family to Frostie?

For the last four years, we've packed the dog and cat in the car and driven to Chino Hills, where my horse is stabled. We've got the setup down to a science: Dale sets the tripod and camera up. I put the dog on a table, then pry the cat out of her carrier and attach her harness and leash. Giving her to Marcus, I get my horse out of her stall.

We then try to take six good pictures, even though Frostie is trying to sniff Katy, who is trying to crawl up Dale's shirt, and Mikey is looking back at me trying to figure out why he's on a table. I'm lucky if everyone is facing the camera; if we're smiling, it's a bonus.

Last year my horse had a baby, so you can imagine the odds of us getting a good shot now. Frostie and baby Snoopy both love Katy, who hates them, Mikey always wants to get in on the action, and the three humans are just trying to control the damage. This year, I brought more film. It took us 14 shots to get everyone facing the camera, but at least most of us are smiling!

A NORMAN ROCKWELL CHRISTMAS

Each Christmas, I have a fantasy about picking the Christmas tree. There is much merriment as my family wanders among the pines, talking and laughing about the trees that are too tall, too short, or remind us of something funny. Afterward, we work together to put the tree in our living room, where we all decorate it. Christmas carols are playing and mugs of hot chocolate interrupt us from time to time.

It's so Norman Rockwell-ian, you could gag. And so different from life with the Carlines.

Our visits to Christmas tree lot start in the driveway, where my husband, Dale, asks, "Where are we going?"

I give him the option of several lots that I've driven past. He looks at me and says, "Where are we going?"

Picking one, I give him directions and we're on our way. Once at the lot, we walk through the rows of trees. I point to a tree and say, "What about this one?"

Dale says, "Okay."

Like most couples, Dale and I have different shopping strategies. I want to review all of the trees, pick a few that we like and choose the best of those. Dale wants to get a tree and go home. After repeated rounds of the above exchange, I finally say, "Let's get this one," and Dale is happy.

Our son, Marcus, has never contributed to these conversations. From the time he could speak and give us his opinion, he has given it freely. When I ask him for his opinion of each tree during this expedition, his answer is the same: a shrug of the shoulders. Apparently, he feels unqualified to judge Christmas trees, although I suspect he feels he knows everything else.

So, our tree picked and paid for, we take it home. Dale puts it in the stand, while I try to help by holding it straight while he tightens the base. This part would go a lot smoother if I would stop letting the tree lean unexpectedly, and if Dale would accept that I can't hear his deep voice and just get a microphone.

I imagine Norman putting his brush down at this point and becoming an accountant.

Dale and Marcus then scamper off and leave me to decorate. I used to try to encourage them to help me, but it never worked. When Marcus was young, he just wanted to sort the ornaments by size, shape and color; now he has important video games to play.

Dale feels that the outside lights are his domain, and their yearly arrangement drains his creativity for any inside decorating.

So I turn on the carols, pour myself a glass of wine and spread the ornaments on the table, after which I make infinite trips to the tree, hanging each ball, each bell, each angel. I reminisce about where I got each one, and what I was doing, and I reflect on where I am now.

And my Norman Rockwell fantasy rekindles for next year.

AN UNWELCOME PRESENT

Whether you celebrate Christmas, Chanukkah, Kwanzaa or Winter Solstice, you know what this season brings. It's that time of year when, in the midst of juggling our job and family and responsibilities and obligations, we have to also squeeze in decorating, shopping, parties and concerts. Working forty hours, preparing meals and running between day care and soccer practices obviously don't keep us busy enough. We also have to stand in line at the post office to send Aunt Mimi her present.

I am in the same boat with everyone else who is running amok during the holidays. I spend hours that I do not have hanging garlands and lights around the house. I bake sugar cookies that I have to ice. A lot of my shopping is done via the Internet, but I still must run to various specialty stores to get stocking stuffers, gift cards for teachers, wine for my hairdresser... the list of activities seems endless.

So when I woke up one Saturday in December with a burning tickle in the back of my throat, I nearly wept. Swallowing handfuls of vitamins and Echinacea, I told myself it was allergies and acted like nothing was wrong. I'm no stranger to Denial; I think my driver's license is still good in that state. So I refused to believe it was a cold.

It couldn't be a cold, because that would throw my Christmas schedule into chaos.

By Saturday night, the thermometer had jolted me back to reality. I had a fever of over one hundred. Sighing, I made the switch from vitamins to Motrin, and from Echinacea to throat lozenges. I may have admitted I had a cold, but I was still going to pump myself full of chemicals and continue with my holiday plans.

By Sunday afternoon, my holiday plans included having my son, Marcus, dig a hole in the backyard and bury me. My fever was up toward one hundred and two, and every muscle in my body ached. No amount of medicine made my headache disappear, and my sleep was interrupted by coughing spasms. There would be no Christmas tree trek today, no baking tomorrow, no trips to the Brea Mall.

I watched my dream of an organized Christmas evaporate in my herbal tea.

It took three days for me to stagger out with my family to get a tree, and another two days to get my baking done. I compromised with my sugar cookies; usually I cut them into a myriad of angels, trees, snowmen and stars. This year, I just went with the trees, baking one big forest.

As far as the shopping goes, it was all done at the very last minute, but not all of it was accomplished.

As I sped through the remaining days, I had to remind

myself that Christmas would come anyway, whether everything was completed or not. And as long as we were all healthy, it would be a very Merry Christmas, indeed.

The Holidays Come Too Soon

I'm writing this column a few days before Thanksgiving, and I'm already surrounded by the sights and sounds of Christmas. KOST Radio is playing non-stop holiday songs, I'm receiving about six catalogs a day in the mail, and there are actually people in Placentia who have Santas on their roofs.

This shouldn't surprise me; I've gotten used to school clothes coming out in June, even though most children have grown out of them by September. And I don't understand why Octoberfest starts in August—aren't 31 days of beer drinking enough? But I still have to ask why we are all in such a hurry. Can't we wait for anything?

This past week, rabid impatience was on display as two new video game consoles were released. Nintendo and Sony dispatched their systems just in time for the holiday rush. And, of course, to establish the appropriate frenzy for the teenage masses, they didn't ship enough units to meet the demand.

After the boxes had left the shelves and the fist fights had subsided, the hysteria traveled over to EBay, where the auctioning began. Out of curiosity, I checked the website. You can buy a $600 Playstation 3 for $1800, or a $250 Wii for $400.

Okay, I confess that it wasn't just curiosity that made me check out the prices.

Marcus wants a Wii.

Sounds like the title of a Dr. Seuss book, but it's actually been the mantra of our house for the past two months. He saved his money, he checked the stores, and prepared for his purchase. On the appointed day, I drove him from store to store, then came home and checked the Internet. It was no use; everyone was completely sold out. Marcus was Wii-less.

Like any normal mom who's used to living life at warp speed, I looked at the auctions, thinking that I could afford to kick in a little money to get Marcus his heart's desire, even if it was over retail.

Then I asked myself why I was in such a hurry. There will certainly be more of these video game systems shipped to our local stores, or available on Amazon. Although they are rivals, Nintendo and Sony want everyone in the world to own both of their systems, even people who have no electricity. They're not going to stop building these things now.

So maybe Marcus will get his Wii by Christmas, or maybe he'll have to wait a little longer. It's even possible that, by the time a new shipment arrives, Marcus' heart will desire something else, although I wouldn't bet on it.

In the meantime, he's being a good sport about it all. And I can't help but think about all of those people bidding outrageous sums of money on EBay, just because they can't wait. In six months, when the shelves are stocked with the newest consoles, will they still feel that they got their money's worth by getting the first box off the boat?

No matter how fast my life is zipping by, I am putting my foot down about the holidays. My Christmas season is not starting until the day after Thanksgiving, no matter how many times I hear "Jingle Bell Rock." And my New Year's resolution this year may be to only drink beer in October.

After all, I can wait.

A VERY MERRY, SOCAL CHRISTMAS

Christmas may be a time of magic, but in southern California, I think our delusions surpass anyone else's in the country.

As I sit at my desk in a tee-shirt and shorts, I'm watching the Santa Ana winds whip my patio umbrella around like a pinwheel, while the radio plays, "Let It Snow." And all I can think of is, yes, please, let it snow, now!

Every year we buy into the dream of a white Christmas while we go dashing through the snow, because, baby, it's cold outside. There are lots of places where this is true. But the reality for us is that Christmas in Placentia is pleasantly warm, unpleasantly hot, or cool and rainy, but definitely not white and fluffy, and not really even cold. The only snow is at Disneyland, and it's artificial. To justify hot cocoa, you have to spend a night watching a soccer game from the metal bleachers at Valencia High School.

I think we should start embracing our environment in our holiday celebrations instead of pretending that Jack Frost is nipping at our noses. And I'm not talking about putting Santa in Bermudas and a Hawaiian shirt. It's cute on Christmas cards, but not realistic. He's traveling all around the world, for goodness' sake; he needs the red suit when he visits, say, Iceland.

I'm just suggesting that we adapt the Christmas trimmings to match our warm weather lifestyles.

For example, we spend a lot of time and money trying to keep pine trees from Oregon alive for a month in our dry, hot weather. And flocking is like telling the world, "Look (wink, wink), it snowed! Here (wink, wink), in southern California!"

Who are we kidding?

Palm trees are more suitable here, although they don't offer enough branches for decorating. How about a Christmas bougainvillea? They have a lot of branches, they grow big as a house, and I haven't been able to kill mine yet, so they must be hardy.

And Christmas carols could be re-written to capture the southern California essence more appropriately. "Let It Snow" could easily be "Let It Blow", "Frosty the Snowman" could become "Crusty the Mud-Boy", and "Sleigh Ride" could turn into "Jet Ski Ride." I've modified "Jingle Bells" to "Jingle Chimes" just to show how easy it would be:

Dashing down the street,
In flip-flops and some shorts,
Chasing down my trashcans,
They're on the neighbors' porch.

Bells on rooftops ring,
Relentless in the wind,
If that noise keeps up this way,
I'm gonna need more gin.

Oh, Jingle Chimes, Jingle Chimes,
Take those #@*% things down!
They've clattered since this morning
And my nerves have run aground! Hey!

Okay, it may not be destined to become a classic. And I probably can't convince anyone to give up their flocked Noble fir in exchange for a Christmas acacia. I guess we'll all just spend another year taking mythical sleigh rides and standing underneath the artificial snow on Main Street.

I'd love to discuss this more, but I have to run out and buy more marshmallows for my cocoa.

KEEPING THE PETS SAFE THROUGH THE HOLIDAYS

Every morning is Christmas morning at our house, except that it's not Santa Claus paying us visits. Instead, it's Santa Chaos—patron saint of pets who sleep all day and play all night. Our dog and cat, Mikey and Katy, are apparently party animals. Katy dances on the tables, Mikey looks for hors d'oeuvres, and I awaken to clean up the damage. Sometimes it's the snack plate left on the coffee table that's now on the floor. Once, my tote bag was looted for vitamins; no one confessed to the crime, but Mikey was very perky that day.

Christmas time holds new possibilities for unauthorized dog treats. For example, a few years ago, I was given a decorative tin shaped like an old-fashioned pie wagon containing Reese's cups. Every year, I refill the tin and place it on the sofa table for family and friends. This morning, I found it, unopened and dented, on the floor, clearly a victim

49

of a toothy hit-and-run.

I've mentioned in a previous column that Mikey is a Corgi, which means he is shaped like an overturned fire hydrant. His legs are so short that if he stands up on the couch, he can't reach over the back cushions to get to anything on the table. Stretching and jumping are also out of the question. Those legs are just too stubby and the body too heavy to get airborne.

Picking up the mess, I had a mental picture of my stumpy dog hurling his body repeatedly over the cushions until he knocked the tin truck onto the floor, then tirelessly chewing the lid in an attempt to open it and indulge in the chocolate-y goodness inside.

It's a good thing he doesn't have thumbs.

Mikey isn't the first dog in my house to have a bottomless stomach and a creative mind. I once had a terrier-mix named Tyler who was both ingenious and obsessive. That dog could find a way into anything edible. Over the 15 years that I owned him, he ate a bag of Oreo cookies, a box of Grape Nuts cereal (without milk!), numerous sandwiches, snacks, and more. When I tried to put him on a diet, he learned to open the pantry door.

Christmas was always a challenge with Tyler. I had to ask if every gift was a food item before I put it under the tree. I forgot one time when the neighbors gave me a pretty package. The next morning, I discovered that they had given me a decorative box of Hershey's Kisses, all of which were gone. They tell you that chocolate is bad for dogs, but Tyler never got that memo.

Then there was the Christmas that I bought some friends a tin of flavored popcorn. Figuring that the popcorn inside was sealed, the tin was sealed, and the whole thing was wrapped in paper, I left it under the tree. The next morning, paper was strewn around the living room like confetti and the can was on its side in the middle of the floor. There were pointy dents around the lid, the mark of my determined pooch. Fortunately, none of the dents broke into the tin and my friends had a good sense of humor.

So, after a life spent with greedy dogs, I know how to handle Mikey's midnight cravings. The Reese's are now on a shelf, away from the sofa and too high for little legs to jump. Because I think Santa Chaos needs to visit someone else for a change.

DECKING THE HALLS AND THE HOUSES

One of the things I love about the holidays is looking at all of the decorated houses as I drive around. From the bright lights to the animated scenes, I am constantly amazed at my neighbors' creativity. And sometimes I am amused.

Some people have a definite theme to their homes. All of the lights are uniform, outlining the roof and windows in white, with twinkles in the trees. There is a lush wreath on the door, and snowflake luminaries lining the sidewalk. You know these people have a lifetime subscription to House Beautiful.

On the other end of the spectrum are the people who just want lights, and lots of them. Every window, every eave, every bush and tree are ablaze with color. Santa and his reindeer dash across the roof, while candy canes form a ring around the Nativity. Reindeer families nod their heads to snowmen, packages and polar bears, in addition to the elves, wise men, and angels that are cavorting on the yard.

Dale loves the excess and I am in awe of the amount of work it takes to install all of the madness—not to mention the electricity bill.

It's interesting to watch all of the fads in holiday decorating. Icicle lights have probably peaked, since they seem to be on every house this year. My childhood in the Midwest has made me a little too conservative when it comes to icicle lights; they must look like icicles to me. White lights are the best, since they are the most realistic. Blue lights are marginal, as ice can take a bluish tint, but I draw the line at red. Snow is not red, rain is not red, so icicles on the roof cannot be red. Let's just say that red lights dripping down a house remind me of something else.

Maybe they should be used at Halloween instead.

Inflatable decorations seem to be really popular now. I've seen everything from Santa to the Nativity, all big and puffy, swaying on lawns. They're okay, but it looks very sad when they deflate. Just yesterday, I saw three snowmen in a yard who were beginning to lose air. They were all huddled together with their heads down, looking like they were either praying or searching for someone's contact lens. I can't imagine how much lower Mary and Joseph could bow their heads over the manger if they sprung a leak.

Actually, I find it interesting how joyfully we display our religious icons during this time of year. Inflatable wise men, oversized menorahs, angels in twinkly lights are all acceptable garden accents during the season. No one worries about whether Frosty the Snowman really visited the Baby Jesus; he still stands by the manger as part of the holiday cheer.

Last year, I saw an intriguing display on Carbon Canyon Road. There is a house on a corner that has a family of plastic deer in their front yard; for Christmas, they added a Nativity scene in front. The problem was that the deer were bigger than the manger, so that it looked like Santa's reindeer were hovering over the Holy Family in a very menacing way. Every time I drove by, I'd imagine a deep-voiced narrator saying, "Due to atomic mutation, Rudolph turned deadly!"

They didn't put their Nativity scene out this year, and I miss it. I'll bet the plastic deer miss it, too.

And how is the Carline house decorated? Dale is in charge of the outside lights, and would love to have a twinkling extravaganza. This year he's taken a minimalist approach, with icicles and blinking stars on the roof and multicolored strands on the bushes. But he dreams of more. Maybe someday we'll join the "excessive" crowd and you'll see angels dancing with polar bears on our lawn.

After all, we don't subscribe to House Beautiful.

CHRISTMAS AT FULL SPEED

Ladies and gentlemen, start your credit cards. Holiday shopping is in full swing.

I usually begin every Thanksgiving by feeling like I'm already running late. The world seems to go into Jingle Bell mode the first of November. Stores have ripped the Halloween candy off of the seasonal aisle and replaced it with tinsel and candy canes. Television is offering made-for-TV specials about Christmas angels and Santa Claus miracles and those "very special" episodes of our favorite shows. Even the radio stations are sneaking carols in between Beyonce and John Meyer.

By Thanksgiving, I'm in a panic, certain that I will not have the house decorated, or the cards mailed, or presents bought by December 25th.

This year, however, I have a new friend,

Amazon.com. Did Marcus just say how much he likes a certain band? I find the band's CD online, press "One Click Ordering" and it's on its way to my house.

Did I catch Dale admiring a friend's electronic gadget? I press "One Click" again, and my wish is Amazon's command.

If I find something nice for my dad, I can even have Amazon wrap it and send it to his house in Illinois. I don't have to see it first. I trust them.

It would be better if Amazon could also write my Christmas letter and send my cards, but at least I don't have to stand in line at the Post Office mailing packages.

I did ask my family for a list so I wouldn't have to follow them around the house listening for hints. Marcus, not surprisingly, sat down immediately and wrote a rather modest list of things he'd like.

Dale was not so prompt.

"What would you like for Christmas?" I emailed him, thinking an email would allow him to type his list in response.

"All I want for Christmas is my two front teeth," he told me, adding a smiley face at the end.

A week later I tried again. "I need your list," I emailed.

"It's only November, for…," he returned.

I didn't know emails could sound so grumpy. I've let the subject go, for now.

In Dale's defense, his favorite day to shop is Christmas Eve. Our family goes to the Brea Mall in the morning, where we follow Dale around, carrying his bags and giving our opinions on whether he should get his brother the brown or blue shirt.

When you like to shop at the last minute, you think

everyone else likes to, too.

So while I wait for Dale to give me his list, I try to get a head start on his shopping. I go through his closet to see what he needs, I check out the Internet for cool toys, and I listen.

Since I have a hard time hearing his soft, low voice, the listening part isn't going too well. The other night, I thought he told me that his basketball team doesn't eat cabbage. Upon further investigation, I found that what he actually said was, "my basketball team doesn't want to scrimmage."

After that, I'm hesitant to buy anything that I've heard him talk about. I can hear it now: "I said running shoes, dear, not rhythm and blues."

But with the help of Amazon, I should be able to get what's on his list, when I get it. Sometime in December, I hope.

JUST A PARTY ANIMAL

What is it about the holiday season that screams, "Let's party"? We spend eleven months of the year in a constant whirlwind of activities. While we're out trying to earn a living 40+ hours a week, we also have to juggle time for our child's recital or sporting event, trips to the doctor and dentist, and, what have I forgotten? Oh, yes, eating and sleeping.

Then when December rolls around, many of us suddenly feel the need to make room in our day for more. We decorate our houses, inside and out, traipse through the mall with the rest of the country, and mail cards to people we never see but pretend we still know. In the midst of this madness, everybody wants to have a party.

And we all want to drop everything and go.

Just next week alone, we are invited to the holiday potluck for the Valencia Choir Department on Monday, then on Saturday we'll be at the Silver Rose Ranch, where my horses are stabled, to have another potluck, and my girlfriend, Jeanne, is talking about having a get-together on some available weekend.

I'm not sure which weekend that will be. Everyone seems to like that middle Saturday. One year, Jeanne told me she wept every time she went to the mailbox in December, because every party invitation was for the same date.

This kind of problem would send Dale into fits. My husband is the quietest man you'll ever meet, but if you invite him to a party, he's there. And when we are invited to two parties for the same night, he's absolutely cranky if we can't attend both.

To add to the chaos, December is also the month that Dale and I usually host a Monday Night Football party for our friends. He makes gumbo, and I make hors d'oeuvres, after giving the house as thorough a scrubbing as possible. We actually have friends who don't know what our house looks like when it's not decorated for Christmas. Apparently, that's the only entertaining we do, at least now that Marcus' schedule rules our lives.

Speaking of Marcus' schedule, in between the decorating and the shopping, we have a few extra activities to squeeze into our days. Last week, he participated in WinterFest, a two-night concert held by all three high school choir departments. Tomorrow, I'm getting up at the most awful hour to help drive the Vocal Jazz group to a school district function. Next week is the Valencia Choir Winter Concert, a one-night event that I have volunteered to run concessions for. We also have tickets to see our friend, Ryan, perform in his winter concert at the Orange County High School of the Arts.

And then—well, you get the picture.

Recently, Marcus brought home an invitation to the Cross Country's year end banquet. He brought the flier home on Tuesday. The banquet was for Thursday.

Now I'm the one who'd like to weep.

So here I sit in the midst of boxes and decorations. We don't have our tree yet, I just got our Christmas cards, and I can't seem to concentrate on getting the stockings hung by the chimney with care. I keep looking at the calendar and repeating, "potluck, concert, potluck, concert, concessions, potluck."

Maybe I do need a party. One with a big glass of wine.

BAD, BAD TREE

This week's column is about when good trees go bad.

We always get a live Christmas tree. I love the smell of fresh pine in the house, and it gives the living room a feeling of energy. Every December, we go to a neighborhood Christmas tree lot, where I indulge in my Norman Rockwell fantasy of a happy, family outing.

It lasts about ten seconds, after which I get out of the car and wander around, with Dale and Marcus trudging behind me, waiting for me to choose a tree.

This year, I was concerned about the dryness of pre-cut trees, so we went to Peltzer Pines out on Rose Drive for a "choose and cut" tree.

Usually, I look at four or five prospects, asking my family what they think of each one. Since Dale's opinion is "yeah, fine," and Marcus' opinion is a shrugged shoulder, I decided to save time this year and get the first acceptable tree I stumbled upon.

Peltzer Pines had many beautifully groomed trees, but each one I approached already had a big, red "Sold" tag hanging on it. I had to look a little farther for a tree that met our requirements—at least six feet tall, not too wide, with at least three good sides (it sits in a corner).

Finally I saw a tree that would work.

"How about this one?" I asked.

Dale walked around, checking the trunk for straightness. "Looks okay," he pronounced.

We paid and took the tree home, where it revealed its true nature.

Dale and Marcus put the tree in the stand while I prepared the living room. This involves clearing the space near the fireplace, putting down a trash can liner to catch any water leaks, and getting out the fishing line.

Due to the Falling Tree Incident of 1995, we now secure our Christmas tree to the wall with fishing line, which is second only to duct tape in its general usefulness.

Marcus brought the tree in and set it in the corner. I wrapped the line around the trunk and told him to let go. The tree leaned out toward him, pulling on the line in my fingers.

That wasn't supposed to happen.

In twelve years, I've never had to hold the tree upright with the fishing line. They always stood up by themselves. The line is just supposed to be insurance.

Marcus and I pushed and pulled and wiggled and juggled that tree, but it would not stand up on its own. Finally, I relented and tied it off at the wall, the line taut and straining.

For once, my son helped me decorate. At fifteen, he still hangs all of the decorations on the same branch, but this year, I let him. In a desperate attempt to make it stand upright, I hung all of the heavy ornaments on the side toward the wall. I hoped the extra weight would bring the tree back to an even balance.

It didn't work.

To top it off, halfway through decorating the tree, my arms began to itch like they were being eaten by a thousand ants. I've never been allergic to my Christmas tree before, but I'm apparently sensitive to this one.

So now we have a decorated tree that careens out from the corner, the star at the top leaning sideways and Marcus' heavily decorated bough stretching toward the middle of the room. The whole effect makes our tree look like I've been watering it with egg nog. I'm hoping it doesn't fall over, because I can't pick it back up without itching, and I'm out of ointment.

I've definitely learned my lesson. Next year, I'm shopping around to find a tree that's more than *acceptable*. In the meantime, I hope this bad tree is good enough to stay upright until Christmas.

GAYLE CARLINE

WHEN GIFT-GIVING WORLDS COLLIDE

When it comes to Christmas shopping, Dale and I are from two different worlds, philosophically. I like to get everything early, so I'm not running amok looking for the sold-out doodad that someone on my list must have. Dale likes to wait until the last possible moment, then hit the mall and buy a bunch of "stuff". His theory is that if he buys enough stuff, sooner or later he'll have something for everyone.

This is why we still have unopened board games and VHS movies in our guest room closet. Dale buys a little too much stuff every year.

His favorite shopping day is Christmas Eve. Yes, every year, we are at the mall on that busiest of days. Dale shops and I provide an extra pair of hands to carry the bags. I try to look helpful, but it's possible the smile on my face is more smug than content. As a matter of fact, I'm certain there

64

is a constant thought bubble above my head, saying, "Ha ha, I'm done and you're not."

I'm also certain that Dale sees it, too, and has figured out how to eradicate it. He has begun to wait until the last minute to give me his Christmas list. Every year it takes longer. First, I ask him. Then I give him my list, to be a good role model. Then the begging begins.

There are a few things I can figure out. Clothes are always a good idea. I know what kind of books he reads, and music he listens to. But without a list, I may overlook that one item he'd never go out and buy for himself. Last year, he asked for a bass—who knew my husband wanted to play music?

This year, every time I ask what he wants for Christmas, he starts singing, "All I want for Christmas is my two front teeth." Maybe he should use last year's present to add a bass line with the song.

Now I think he has encouraged Marcus to drag his feet about his list. When I asked our son what he wants this year, he gave me a surprising response: a blank stare. I couldn't understand it. Being a typical kid, he usually hands me his list before I ask for it.

Most years, I can figure out what he wants, but this year is a mystery. He has an iPod, a laptop, two guitars, a Wii, in other words, an embarrassment of riches. What do we get for him?

When Marcus still had Toys R Us tastes, Dale and I would shop for his presents together. It was the only time Dale would shop early for anything. As Marcus' list matured, I became the sole purchaser, ordering from Amazon, and chasing down Wii's. Perhaps Dale has enlisted Marcus to help him return to the time when we shopped together for his gifts.

He could have just asked me, earlier.

In the past, there was one card I could play that would get a list from my two men. "Either tell me what you want for Christmas," I'd say, "Or you're getting socks and underwear." I usually save this for the last threat, right after the shameless begging.

It's mid-December and I've already used it. Marcus rolled his eyes. Dale said, "Yay, socks and underwear!"

Good thing Hanes doesn't sell out.

ITCHING FOR A CHRISTMAS TREE

This may be the last year of a live Christmas tree in our house, which makes me very sad. I love the smell of real pine during the holidays, plus it seems to give the room an extra energy, but I seem to have developed an allergy.

Last year, our tree made my skin itch whenever I touched it. I assumed it was a bad tree, since it also leaned at an awkward angle. This year, we returned to Peltzer Pines and carefully chose a nice, straight tree. It looks very pretty in our living room, sandwiched between the white brick fireplace and the stereo cabinet.

Unfortunately, every time I get near it, my skin erupts in a fury of red, burning dots that I want to scratch to the point of madness. This means last year's tree, while physically unruly, was not as bad as I thought. My skin is the culprit.

Our family has specific chores for holiday decorating.

Dale handles the outdoor lights. Every year, he attempts to make our house the twinkling extravaganza of his dreams. I'm responsible for indoor decorating, including the tree, the stockings on the mantle, and the lighted candy canes over the kitchen sink. This means I must decorate a tree that makes me break out in a rash.

By the way, Marcus's job is to perform any requested task as slowly as possible, until it seems easier to just do it without him.

I mentioned this new allergy to an online group, Twitter. A friend cautioned me, "Don't do it! You could go into anaphylactic shock!" I hadn't thought of that, but I told her I was planning to wear long sleeves and gloves. "That will help, but take some Benedryl, too," she ordered.

Here's the thing about Benedryl and me—when I take it, I can't stay awake. I can remain semi-conscious if I'm moving, but as soon as I sit down, I am out. I certainly cannot drive after I've taken one. So I might be able to get the tree decorated as long as I work quickly. If I pause to adjust an ornament on a branch, I might just end up leaning against the trunk, snoring.

I might have to press Marcus into service, although I fear I might develop an allergic reaction to so much nagging.

Next year, what will I do? Perhaps we should get one of those energy-saving, environmentally-friendly, artificial trees, although it will depress me. You can call them artificial, but I know what they are—fake. How can I celebrate a real holiday with a fake tree? I know, it's semantics. I also know I'll get over it, by reminding myself that I'm saving the environment, conserving energy, and sparing myself a possible hospital trip.

Back in the 60's, my grandmother got a fake tree. It

was aluminum, about five feet tall and silver. The manufacturer didn't even try to pretend that it might be real. The best part was the color wheel, a stand-alone light box with a rotating lens of three or four colors. The aluminum tree would reflect the color as the wheel rotated around. In addition, the color wheel was musical, and played a couple of Christmas carols in a high, tinny sound that made you develop an eye twitch after about ten minutes.

I'm thinking, maybe I should find one of those on eBay and "recycle" it to our house. After all, if it's got to be an artificial tree, why not go fake all the way?

GAYLE CARLINE

For Me? I Love It!

I keep seeing a commercial on TV that bothers me with each successive viewing. A man and woman sit on a couch. He keeps opening Christmas presents, each more unwanted than the last, while the woman (I'm assuming it's his wife) sits and smiles.

The announcer tells us that the poor gal should break down and get him "what he wants this Christmas", as if she hasn't been trying very hard. I can't even remember what he wanted, but it wasn't a unicorn statue.

All through the holidays, we are being admonished, not only to give others what they want, but to make certain our heart's desires are under the tree on Christmas morning. The focus is on the present. It must make the recipient's dreams come true, or don't bother wrapping it.

Picking out a perfect gift has become such a weighty

decision that many people have surrendered to gift cards. Gift cards are sensible. They are practical. They are also less time consuming than wandering through stores and agonizing over what color sweater he'd like, or whether she'll like this artist's CD.

What concerns me about this is a feeling of intimidation as the gift giver. What if I don't fulfill their every whim? What if my present isn't exactly what they want? The stress is enough to send me running for the gift cards, and the extra-strength egg nog.

What happened to a gracious recipient? I'm not talking about people who curl up their noses at the blue iPod because they asked for the white one. We won't discuss them, except to say, if coal wasn't so expensive, I'd like to see it in their stockings. I'm talking about giving unconditional thanks for whatever you're given.

Every year, my nieces spend their own money, probably at some little thrift shop, to purchase a gift for me. It is usually a figurine, or bubble bath, or some other little trinket. It's never something I asked for, and not anything I need, but I adore their present. They searched through a store, thinking about me, and spent their own money. I may get a unicorn statue, but their real present to me each year is their thoughtfulness.

Recently, I received a present from one of my students. The ten-year old girl made me a muffler out of felt squares. She selected a pattern with horses on it, just for me. It looks cute and crafty, and very homemade, which is not my style, but I will wear it at the ranch whenever it's cold. I cherish this present because my student made it for me.

After all, I'm pretty sure that Mary didn't tell the wise men, "Um, myrrh? Here's the thing—we could really use some diapers."

If Mary's not a good role model, then who is?

So even though I'd like to find a Kindle under the tree from Santa, I will be thankful for any and all my presents. To be in the hearts of loved ones, to have people think of me, is the real gift I will celebrate. Hopefully, the presents I give out will be received in that same manner.

By the way, my presents do include a few gift cards for a few people this year. But it's only because that's what they want.

SNEEZING FOR TRADITION

The holiday season is in full swing, and at our house, Christmas is coming up fast. Between all of our normal festivities, I'm also squeezing in choir duties and book signings, and I am behind schedule on everything.

This includes getting our tree. We like a live tree, and for years, we traipsed through the various lots all over the city, trying to pick one that would last two weeks without drying out so badly I was afraid of turning on the lights. Dale likes to leave the decorations up until his birthday, which is January 2nd, so getting a tree that will stay reasonably green is important.

Finally, we discovered Peltzer Pines' Choose and Cut lot and have been getting fresh trees that last about a month before I get nervous.

Last year, I discovered something new about myself;

I'm allergic to Christmas trees. Whenever my skin brushes the needles, it erupts in itchy, red bumps. I started breaking out two years ago, but at the time, I thought the tree had been treated with some kind of chemical. When it happened again last year, I realized it was my problem, not the tree's. I still decorated, but I had to cover myself so my skin did not touch pine.

Do you know how hard it is to hang ornaments with gloves on?

For the first time ever, this year I have been contemplating an artificial tree. It would make less work for me. I wouldn't need to worry about watering it every day. We could leave it up until Dale's birthday without a second thought. Heck, we could leave it up until Marcus' birthday in October.

If we got one of those trees that already has the lights on it, I wouldn't even have to untangle the miles of light strings and spend an hour trying to wrap them around in an even pattern. Plus, I wouldn't have to do it with disposable gloves duct-taped to my sweatshirt. It would be a win-win, except...

Except that, for me, part of Christmas is finding the right tree. Not the perfect tree, the right one. Maybe it's the "Charlie Brown Christmas" effect, but I don't want a straight, perfectly shaped tree that will be the same, year after year. I want a tree with personality.

We've had trees that leaned this way and that, with branches too weak to hold more than a feather, much less any ornaments. Tree tops have been hit or miss; either our "Las Vegas Star of Bethlehem" fits on the topmost point or I have to get creative with fishing line, or more duct tape.

No matter what kind of tree we get, fishing line will

be involved, as we tie the tree to the wall every year. When Marcus was four, our tree fell over. This happened at the most inconvenient time, of course, early in the morning. I was trying to get ready for work and Dale was on travel. In my sleepy stupor, I fixed it by hammering a nail into the wall and anchoring the tree with fishing line.

It's become our tradition.

So, even though an artificial tree would make more sense, we will be shopping at the Choose and Cut lot again this year. I'll be breaking out the disposable gloves and untangling lights, which will be wrapped around the tree in a good top-to-bottom twinkle ratio. Hopefully, the branches will support all of the mismatched trinkets that remind me of Christmases past.

What I really hope is that we get our tree soon. I don't want to spend Christmas day scratching.

STOPPING TO ENJOY THE SHOW

Even though my Christmas season is moving at warp speed, I've decided this year to stop running amok long enough to enjoy a few holiday activities.

For example, I'm going to the Celtic Christmas program tonight at the Placentia Library. I volunteered last year and had a great time. Being of Celtic ancestry, I felt a special affinity for the music, as well as the words of Dylan Thomas.

Last week, I went to the Christmas tree lighting ceremony at the Placentia Civic Center. I confess, this was my first year to attend. Every year, I see the announcement and wish I could go, but there's always been something else on my schedule. Afterward, I read about the event in the paper, look at the pictures, and regret not being there.

So when I saw the tree would be lit on a night when I

was free, I entered it on my calendar and waited impatiently.

When Friday night came, I dressed in my warmest clothes. The Civic Center is a few blocks from my house, and I had this Norman Rockwell fantasy of walking over to the event with Dale and Marcus, then having dinner at the IHOP across the street.

That fantasy didn't last long. Dale had to work late, and said he'd try to make it to the ceremony. Marcus was home, lying on the couch and twiddling his cell phone. Every few minutes, he'd stop and text something to someone.

"I'm going to the tree lighting ceremony at the Civic Center," I told him.

His response was concise, if unclear. "Hrmph."

"Would you like to walk down and watch it with me?"

"Uhhhh… noooo."

"Fine. I'll take the dog." I put the leash on Mikey, who was overjoyed at the prospect of going for walkies, and we strolled into the night air.

Mikey was agreeable company, although our walk was slowed considerably by his need to stop at every tree, and there would be no trip to IHOP unless I could convince them he was a seeing-eye dog. His short stature made that unlikely.

When we got to the event, Mikey wasn't the only dog there. He exchanged sniffs with a couple of rescued greyhounds, sporting red winter jackets, and some huskies decked out in Christmas lights. I made a note to dress Mikey up a little next year if he accompanies me again.

The program was really fun, and lovely. Choirs sang, children danced, and Santa made a guest appearance. I was especially impressed by the Placentia Community Chorus, but my favorite part of the evening was when the artificial snow blew around and the children got so excited. It's possible they were more excited by the snow than Santa's arrival.

Dale joined me while a Brownie troop read "Twas the Night Before Christmas." We talked to some Valencia parents, as well as Al Shkoler, who wanted to know if Mikey has ever made the column.

"Only when he's done something bad," I said.

At the end of the festivities, Dale walked back to his car, while Mikey and I walked home. Marcus was in the same position on the couch where we left him.

"You should have come," I told him. "There were some Valencia kids there."

"Hrmph," he replied.

Oh, well, I may not be able to get him to any of the town festivities, but I'll be at the library in time to get a good seat for the show. Too bad I won't be able to bring Mikey. He may be a Welsh Corgi, but he's got two legs too many for the event.

ALL OF THE HOLIDAY SEASON IN ONE DAY

The holidays remind us of how thankful we are, and how blessed we are. They also remind us of how busy we are. No matter what we pack into our normal day, in December, we manage to squeeze in one more activity… or two… dozen.

Usually, all of my activities are spread from Thanksgiving through Christmas. This year, however, they are all jammed into the same week. I feel like I'm in the middle of speed-Christmas.

The week began with the Valencia High School Choir Winter Concert. As president of the booster club, I spent time delegating tasks, answering questions, and making lists of things we needed to make the evening enjoyable for students and their families. The planning culminated on Tuesday, when one of the parents called, frantic that she could not find the coffee urn she had promised to lend.

"No problem," I told her. "We'll go to Plan B."

I truly didn't want her to worry (she's going to worry enough about where her urn is), but I didn't have a Plan B. A trip to Sam's Club was on my list, so I swung through their restaurant supply aisle. They had a 60-cup urn for a fairly low price; I thought that was an excellent solution to the problem. The choir uses a coffee urn for enough performances that it would be worth it.

The day was still young when I took it home and washed it out, like the instructions said. That's when I discovered something unpleasant: the urn's spigot leaked. I took it apart and put it together several times before calling their customer service number. I was pretty sure it was missing a washer to seal the connection.

"Is there supposed to be a washer?" I asked.

"Is there a washer?" the representative countered.

"No. Is there supposed to be one?"

"Does it have one?"

This continued for three more rounds before he admitted, yes, it needed a washer and he'd be happy to mail me one, which would have been lovely if I didn't need it that night.

Instead, I schlepped back to Sam's to exchange the urn.

My tasks were eventually completed, my volunteers showed up at the concert to help, and everyone had a good time. I wish I could have reveled in the moment, but the very next morning, I had to drive several members of the Vocal Jazz group to the Alta Vista Country Club, where they sang at the Rotary Club Breakfast.

Can I confess that I am not a morning person? Nevertheless, I managed to shower, dress, and find my car keys in time to get Marcus and another student to the country club by 6:45.

The Rotarians were kind enough to invite the kids (and their chaperones) to stay for breakfast. They were even so gracious as to let the students go through the buffet line first, although I worried about the wisdom of this. There are fifteen students in the group, five of which are teenaged boys, a term synonymous with "perpetual eating machines."

Ultimately, we managed to drag them away from the bacon and eggs, and get them to school. There was no time to relax, however, as I had to run home and prepare fundraising flyers to hand out before winter break, and confirm my other chaperone for Friday's choir event at the school district's holiday luncheon.

In addition to these performances, I have a holiday party to attend, a luncheon with friends, and tickets to a Christmas play. I'm thankful for all of the celebrations, but I may have to schedule time to count my blessings.

THINKING OF THE FUTURE

I write this column a week and a day before it is published, which means I have to check the calendar and make certain my writing is topical. So I'm sitting in my recliner, two days from Christmas, nursing a cold, and trying to write a column about ushering in the New Year. Unfortunately, all I can think about is that tomorrow is Christmas Eve, I still have some shopping to do, and that colds are given to us by malicious pixies who like to spoil our holidays.

Another aspect of having to write this column early is that I'm counting on life to continue as I expect. I suppose it's an optimistic view, to write as though the New Year is upon us and nothing dire will happen in the next week to stop it.

The process backfires, occasionally. I wrote about planning to go to the Celtic Christmas Program at the Placentia Library a few weeks ago. I really wanted to go, and made arrangements with Dale to get Marcus to his guitar lesson. On the night of the event, I got a sinus headache that made me want to pound my head on the wall because nothing could make it feel worse. I spent the evening as far away from noise as possible.

But I will pretend that New Year's Eve is upon us, followed by the first day of 2010. Is it ironic that we associate the Eve with partying, and New Year's Day with resolving not to overindulge?

My personal belief is that every day, we should take stock of what we're doing and why. That way, if we've wandered off the track, we can correct our course immediately. Still, I suppose there should be some end-of-the-year accounting for how we did. Perhaps we need some distance to realize that our year-long fascination with unusual diets (no carbs, no protein, grapefruit soup, etc.) haven't been as successful as we'd like.

Looking back over a year also shows us how really important things turned out to be rather trivial, given enough time. Just fan through last January's gossip magazines if you want proof.

My family plans to be in Idyllwild with friends for New Year's Eve. We will have a quiet evening of talk, maybe some games, and if we're lucky, a little snow. Some of us may steal a moment to think about what we'll do differently next year. I'd like to give you my resolution list now, but I don't know what it is yet. I suppose I'll resolve to keep doing the right things and do the wrong things differently, just for a change.

In the meantime, I shall assume that Dale and Marcus and I spent a wonderful day on Christmas Eve, shopping at the Brea Mall, watching the snow fall at Disneyland, and having dinner in Downtown Disney. For the record, we go to the Brea Mall so Dale can finish his shopping. I buy the Cinnabons, and serve as his schlepper, taking packages to the car so he can continue to look for more things.

On Christmas Day, we had our morning time with presents and Cinnabons, then enjoyed tamales with our friends, the Mesa family, before heading to Dale's mom's house for turkey and more presents.

By the time this column is published, I'll also have spoken at the La Habra Public Library, about why I used Placentia as the setting for my novel, what changes I made to the town, and why.

Perhaps my pre-New Year's resolution is to kick those malicious cold-pixies to the curb so they don't spoil all this fun.

TO OUR HOUSE, WITH LOVE, FROM US

I remember the Christmases of my childhood as being exercises in excess. Each year, the tree fairly exploded with presents. My parents weren't rich. They just bought lots of little gifts and wrapped them all individually. I got coloring books, crayons, mittens, socks, and so forth.

In my own family, I've continued this tradition. If the packages don't extend from under the tree by at least two feet, I haven't shopped enough.

This year, I'm not as frenzied about buying things. Dale has all the clothes he'll ever need, and most of the electronic toys he wants. Marcus' list has gotten shorter, consisting of a couple of video games and a musical instrument. I don't need any new clothes, bric-a-brac is just more stuff to dust, and believe it or not, I have enough shoes.

Don't yell at me about the shoes. If your world

revolved around your house and the stables, all you'd need are fuzzy slippers, tennis shoes, and boots. Check, check, and check.

I was thinking of suggesting to Dale that, instead of exchanging presents, we do something nice for the two of us. Now that we are not tied to Marcus' schedule, we could take a weekend trip somewhere. Or perhaps we could get something for both of us to enjoy, like a new TV for the family room.

The car and the house must have read my mind.

Last week, I pulled into the doctor's office and noticed large clouds of white smoke pouring from under my minivan's hood. I went to my appointment, worrying the entire time about what was wrong. I'm glad the technician was doing a thorough job with my ultrasound, but I wanted her to hurry so I could call my mechanic. At last, she finished filming the mini-series, and I rushed outside and started making calls.

The good news was it was a $40 part that broke in my heating system. The bad news was Allen either had to take the car apart or become a contortionist to fix it. God love him, he bent his fingers in a million different ways, to save his time and my money.

It was still an expensive Christmas gift for the minivan. I was thinking of something smaller, like an air freshener. Now there was a couple hundred dollars less to spend on a weekend trip or flat-screen TV.

Then there was the fence. Like most people, we have a wooden fence between the block wall and our house. Ours has been in a fragile state for quite some time and we planned to replace it in January. The recent high winds moved our plan up by a few weeks.

I came home yesterday and saw the side of the house as I pulled into the drive. Thinking someone had left the gate open, I walked around to close it and discovered the gate was still closed. It was just on the ground, with the rest of the fence. The winds had blown it down.

The bad news is, when I went to Home Depot to get an estimate for rebuilding the fence, I found that our current, dilapidated wood was not standard. If we want to re-create what we had, they're all specialty cuts, as in more expensive. The good news is, as I was standing at the help desk being given an estimate, three contractors gave me their cards.

It's not as much fun as a trip or a TV, but I guess it fits the description of a gift for both of us. Maybe Dale would like mittens instead.

WHEN THE SHINE WEARS OFF

Not only am I Facebook friends with Marcus, I'm buddies with many of his high school pals as well. It's been fun to see their posts about adjusting to college life. Recently, one of his friends, who is going to college in Chicago, posted her excitement about seeing her first snowfall.

Having spent twenty-four years of my life in Illinois, I couldn't resist commenting: "I want to see the same excitement from you in March, when there's already 3 feet of snow on the ground—dirty, crunchy, old, stale snow."

It occurred to me the holiday season is much like that.

There's the feeling of exhilaration after Thanksgiving as I realize the Christmas season has officially begun. We will pick out a tree and decorate it, select gifts, and attend parties and concerts. I can almost smell the holiday spices in the air.

Oh, wait, that's potpourri at the grocery store

entrance.

My family visits the choose-and-cut tree lot, excited to pick out a tree. Actually, I'm the one skipping through the pines, while Dale and Marcus follow along. They're happy about selecting a tree, but they might as well carry a sign that says, "Just Pick One, Mom."

The smell of a fresh pine tree in the living room makes the entire house feel alive. Of course, over the past few years, I've become more and more allergic to the needles, but I can still enjoy hanging angels on the branches, even if my sleeves are duct-taped to my gloves.

Unpacking the decorations makes me feel a little giddy. It's almost better than opening presents, because it's like seeing old friends. As I decorate, each ornament on the tree makes me reminisce about the person who gave it to me.

Once the house is decorated, I celebrate by sitting in the living room with just the Christmas lights twinkling, and have a cup of tea, or maybe some hot cocoa. I go over my list of gifts to purchase and cookies to bake, and make my plans. It is a perfect moment.

By Christmas Eve, the moments are not so perfect anymore.

Ceramic snowmen and Santas may be cute, but I grow tired of dusting them all. After the first week, I've also grown tired of chasing the cat off the festive tablecloths, so I'm reduced to picking the extra cat hair off the red plaid and washing them if we have company.

Our beautiful tree accepts less and less water every day, no matter what kind of super-freshening formula I've used. I pull on the needles, which don't come off in my hand, but after a couple of weeks, they feel so dry I'm afraid to turn on the lights. Gone are the nights of sitting in the twinkling lights with a cup of tea. I'm too busy running to concerts and parties, anyway, as well as doing last minute shopping.

Last minute shopping means last minute wrapping. Early in the season, my packages have sharp edges and pretty ribbons. By Christmas Eve, everything is going in a gift bag. If they're lucky, they get a poof of tissue paper on top. If I'm tired, there's not even a tag—just a name written in Sharpie on the side.

By the day after Christmas, the holiday looks like December's snowfall in March. Opened presents are strewn everywhere in our house, not to mention dirty dishes, as well as three tired people.

Still, like the first snowfall, we can look back on that first day of the holiday season and say, "Whee!"

An Evolving Tradition

No matter what you are celebrating this month, I'm guessing everyone has traditions, involving family and friends, food and events. You never know how many customs you've developed for the holidays until they start to slip away.

When Marcus went to college, people kept asking me if I was adjusting to an empty nest, but I really didn't feel anything except pride and happiness that our son was doing so well at Long Beach.

Of course, I did notice no one took out the trash anymore, but I arm-wrestled Dale to see who assumed that task. I lost.

Then the Christmas season came along and exposed the empty chair at the Carline table. I knew there were a lot of things done as a family. But I had no idea how much Marcus' absence would affect me.

For example, every year, the three of us picked out a tree. We usually went to the 'Choose and Cut' lot, since Dale likes to keep the tree up past his birthday on January 2nd and I like to avoid fire hazards in my house. Suddenly this year, I realized it would be a two-person job. There was a small window of opportunity on a Sunday afternoon to get it done, until Dale had a change of schedule.

"I need to hang the lights at my mom's house," he told me. "Can you go get a tree?"

I hadn't picked out a tree by myself since I was single, but I drove to the lot on Rose Drive, rolled the minivan slowly across the gravel, and went on a solo hunt. I'd like to whine that there was no one to help me choose, but neither Dale nor Marcus ever helped in that way. They were just along for the muscle. Our usual routine was that I'd stop at a tree and say, "What do you think of this one?" Dale would say, "It's fine. Let's get it." Marcus would shrug his shoulders. It's as if they conspired to make me choose the tree anyway.

As I stood in the middle of the forest, I missed their lack of opinions. I also missed their relative heights. Without them, I had no real idea what size tree to get. I was trying to get a seven-foot tree, but they all seemed to be sold. When you're just a smidgeon over five feet tall, a six foot tree looms large.

The one I finally picked is only six feet tall if we could put it in four-inch heels instead of a stand.

The result of having a markedly smaller tree is that I couldn't put all the ornaments on it. As I decided what would go on the branches and what would stay in the box, I began to feel a little misty about the ornaments Marcus had made as a child.

That led me to question all the decorations I put up

every year. There is the garland that Marcus always helped me string. We have an Advent Calendar with the Christmas story, all in 24 little books. Marcus used to read a book each night, then hang it on the garland. This year, Marcus would not be here to hang the garland or read the story. He would arrive just in time to see the results.

In the blink of an eye, our family tradition of togetherness was changed into a tradition of preparing the house for our son. The things we did together are now my way of showing him that nothing has changed.

After all, the holidays are all about traditions, right?

PRESENTS FROM THE KIDS

It's the beginning of December. If you haven't gotten your holiday shopping done by now, forget it. The latest gadgetry and hot, new toy is sold out. The most you can hope for is that your aunt will like the camouflage Snuggie the stores overstocked because they thought it would be the most popular color.

For your sake, I hope your aunt isn't a pacifist.

Actually, these days, it's easy to fall back on gift cards. Some people get them first, before even trying to find out what anyone wants. Grocery stores sell them, so you can get the Christmas ham and the iTunes card in the same trip.

Pretty soon, we won't decorate our trees with ornaments, we'll just hang cards.

When I was young, my parents didn't have a lot of money, but they wanted Christmas to be an extravaganza, so our tree was stuffed with inexpensive gifts. Everything was wrapped individually, so that you'd get a pair of gloves in one box, then the matching scarf in another.

I'm surprised we didn't have to train for the unwrapping marathon.

My parents got a couple of presents apiece. Usually, they would stick our names on one of the packages, although I don't remember going shopping. One year, my dad thought it would be fun if my younger brother, Randy, helped wrap presents for Mom. Randy carried the first present out to the living room and handed it to her.

"Here's your gloves," he said.

Did I mention he was three years old?

She tried to ignore him and told him to put the presents under the tree. A few minutes later, he came out of the bedroom with the second present.

"Here's your purse to go with your gloves," he announced on his way to the tree.

It might have been great Father-Son bonding, but it wasn't much of a surprise for Mom on Christmas.

As I recall, this was also the year my brother pulled the fully-decorated, lights-blazing, tree over on himself, so it was the Randy trifecta of Christmases at our house.

I used to try to get Marcus to shop with me for Dale's present. When he was very little, he didn't understand what Dad might want, so I had to choose for him. As he grew older, he couldn't decide what Dad might want, so I had to choose for him. Once he became old enough to handle money, I chose to let him do it.

We've gotten some interesting gifts since then. I love that he puts so much thought into what he thinks we like.

Last weekend, we went to Marcus' fall vocal jazz

concert. The students gave their director a gift at the end of the evening. As she opened it, I thought perhaps they had stuffed a rabbit in a plastic bag. It turns out, they had given her a "spirit hood", which is a furry hat that looks like an animal, with long ears that can be used as mittens. She was ecstatic and tried it on immediately.

I kept thinking she looked like an anime creature from a show Marcus used to watch.

After the concert, I told Marcus how much I enjoyed his performance, and the show.

"I love you, Sweetie," I added. "But I don't want one of those spirit hood things for Christmas."

"Oh, but you should have one, Mom. They're everywhere. Anyone can wear them."

If I'm lucky, he'll save his shopping until the last minute, and they'll be sold out. If not, look for me around town. I'll be the old lady with the rabbit on her head.

THE CARD'S IN THE MAIL

Christmas comes with many traditions, both universal and personal. Most people decorate trees, but not everyone leaves Aunt Whoosit's marble cake out for Santa. One tradition most of us engage in is both easy and difficult, subject to delight and ridicule.

I'm talking about Christmas cards.

Most people think Christmas cards were invented by a certain greeting card company as a way of getting us to buy their merchandise, but that's not true. They were invented by a postal worker in England who wanted to find new ways for people to use this newfangled "post office" system.

One way or the other, it was all about the money.

Still, I like to receive Christmas cards. There are friends and relatives I rarely see, and it's nice to get a card from them. For one thing, I know they're still alive. I don't always get news about elderly relatives back in Illinois. I especially like when they've included a personal note.

I like to send cards, too. In my youth, I'd visit the card shop, choose a package of cards I liked, then sign them, stamp them, and send them on their way. I usually wrote a little something about how I was doing and hoped they were well.

Didn't Aunt Betty deserve more than "Love, Gayle" on a card once a year?

Then I married Dale and we had Marcus and I started down that slippery slope of including pictures. We began at one of those one-hour places in the mall, in front of a picture of a Christmas tree. That was followed by years of posing in front of the fireplace with the dog and cat. Then I got a horse and we moved the chaos to the ranch.

At some point, I decided that including a picture in the card was not as efficient as having a picture that was the card. This meant sending the picture to the drug store, and hoping the cards turned out the way you planned.

On more than one year, I was surprised by the slightly enlarged photo, clearly showing the dog's closed eyes, the drool on baby Marcus' shirt or the extra wrinkle on my neck from tilting my head the wrong way.

Once I had mastered the art of getting everyone in the room for a photo, there was one more hurdle to cross: the Christmas letter. As I wrote the same words in every card, I started thinking, maybe I should write it once and make copies. I kept my first one short and light. It got a good response, so I've kept writing.

This year, I got another idea. If I could combine the picture and the letter on one piece of paper, it would be better than sending a letter folded into a card. I found brochure paper at the office supply store and fashioned a card with a picture on the front, and the letter on the inside.

The best part was, I could do it all on my own printer and save both money and time, since I would not have to wait for my cards to be shipped to me. It was genius.

Unfortunately, my printer hated it.

The weight of the brochure paper was unpleasant for the printer to grab. More than three or four copies made it growl, stop, and tell me it was out of paper. After several rounds of fighting, I was reduced to hand-feeding single sheets to the printer. What I saved in money, I spent in time.

I had to do it, though. It's Christmas tradition.

MEMORIES HIDDEN IN THE ORNAMENTS

This is the time of year when many people take a look at their life and reflect. Have they done enough? Have they met their goals?

Would Clarence the angel tell them they've had a Wonderful Life?

I'm one of those reflective types. For me, it begins when I start unpacking the boxes of Christmas decorations, which Dale gets down from the garage rafters and puts in the living room. He always deposits them where the tree goes, so I have to move them.

I keep thinking I should stop grumbling and ask him to put them somewhere else, but after seventeen years, the grumbling feels like tradition.

In my youth, I wanted a "theme" tree of all blue and white, or just angels, etc. I was too poor to afford such a tree, so I handmade some decorations, and was given others. After all these years, I've decided I prefer a tree decorated with memories, a tree with a personality.

Our tree has so much personality, it should either be on a stage or a psychiatrist's couch.

As I unwrap each ornament, I think about how I acquired it. I have the very first ornament I was given, when I was six years old. Then there is the set of wooden ornaments I hand-painted from a kit, along with some dough creations I made the Christmas I was out on my own and broke. Also there are the many angels I received from friends when I was a flying angel in the Glory of Christmas.

Let's face it, I try to be a sassy gal, but I'm sentimental at heart.

Last year, Marcus wasn't around to help decorate, but he was home to help me take everything down. As we removed the ornaments from the tree, I pointed to the ones I had gotten for him over the years, the "Baby's 1st Christmas" and "Thomas the Tank Engine."

"Someday you'll be in your own place and have your own tree. These can be your starter kit."

He didn't even glance at them. "Nah, that's okay."

I was momentarily stunned. This was the son who couldn't get rid of his baby toys because Samirah had given them and he didn't want to forget her. He still is the boy who can't part with his childhood books, including Goodnight, Moon.

"Well, are there other ornaments or decorations you'd rather have instead?" I asked.

"Not really." He was so quick, so dismissive, I nearly asked to see his I.D.

This year, his words came back to me, and their

meaning became clear. I was the only one who cared about my first ornament, or his. When I am no longer here, all of the angels and bells and crazy little figurines will lose their sentimental value. They will be things to be disposed of, somehow.

With my luck, they'll end up on eBay and sell for a fortune.

I admit, I felt a little melancholy as I hung the ornaments on the tree. In the middle of my decorating, a writer friend called and caught me at my lowest.

"I care about your first ornament," she said, and we laughed, because she's never even seen my house.

We decided that someday, Marcus will marry and my daughter-in-law will want his first ornaments. After all, that's the way it is with my brother. It's his wife, Mindy, who treasures the family keepsakes.

Barring that, we made a plan. I'm going to put in my will, that Marcus must keep the decorations or forfeit his inheritance. That should give him something to reflect about.

A REALLY BIG CHRISTMAS

After I moved to southern California, I flew home to Illinois for Christmas the first year. The weather rewarded me with a blizzard, trapping me in Decatur until New Year's Day.

It was only one of the reasons I learned my lesson and now do my celebrating in Placentia.

The other reason was, I came home with excess baggage. For years, I had asked for two items for Christmas: a picnic basket and a sleeping bag. For years, I had received other nice gifts instead. That year, however, I walked into my parents' house and saw three enormous boxes for me under the tree, all swathed in a jumble of wrapping paper, haphazardly taped and wrinkled.

Now that I lived two thousand miles away, my parents decided a picnic basket and sleeping bag would be excellent gifts. They would be so easy for me to schlep through an airport.

In addition, my mother was into making dolls that year. She made me a Little Orphan Annie doll, which was cute, but was also three feet tall. No matter how I tried, it didn't fit into the suitcase, meaning I would have to carry her home.

Try to imagine a young woman with curly red hair hefting a large doll with curly red hair through the airport terminal and onto the plane. At one point, I tried to stuff my doppelganger in the overhead compartment. The flight attendants were horrified, and made me put her in the empty seat next to me.

I was thinking of this while I wrapped Dale's presents this year. Normally, I nag him for the first two weeks of December until he finally gives me some ideas for gifts he would like. This year, he spilled the beans early. He wanted a toolbox.

Not just any toolbox, though, he explained. He wanted the large kind with drawers that pull out, but not the kind on wheels because he doesn't have room for that. This was described with hand gestures and pointing to a TV show where someone was in their garage looking for a screwdriver.

I wondered, if I got Dale a big toolbox, would all our missing screwdrivers return from their hiding places?

Lucky for me, Sears was having a half-price sale on that kind of toolbox. Luckier still, they had a 255-piece tool set for half-price, too. I didn't know if Dale needed 255 more tools, but I knew I could always use one of the 16 screwdrivers in the set.

Marcus helped me move them into the spare bedroom, where I spent a good thirty minutes trying to wrap one large heavy box and one medium, heavier box, with a handle. The room is not large and already has furniture, so there was not a lot of maneuvering space. I had to shift the large box, standing it on each end, and rolling it side to side, in an effort to tape Christmas paper on it.

It was less like gift wrapping and more like yoga positions.

I thought the smaller, lumpy gift would be easier, until I realized, if I wrapped the handle, it would be too heavy to pick up without future back surgery. I carefully cut the paper to expose the handle so I could put it under the tree later.

As I wrestled the boxes, I thought about the large, lumpy packages under my parents' tree long ago, and marveled that either of my folks was limber enough to get any paper around them.

I was also thankful we don't have to get these packages to the airport.

NEVER MIND TRADITIONS, JUST ADAPT

Thanksgiving is over and done, which means we have begun that mad dash toward Christmas, or Hanukkah, or Kwanzaa, or maybe just madness in general. There are gifts to be purchased, decorations to be hung and parties galore.

After all, we've got plenty of time in our schedules for this, right?

Like most families, we have our traditions, but lately the things we've "always done" can't be done anymore, due to changing circumstances. This year we may have a brand new kind of Christmas.

Marcus got a job recently, singing in a church choir in San Pedro. Color me naïve, but I was surprised to learn that some choirs pay some members. He's apparently in charge of the bass section, leading them through rehearsal on Thursday evenings, then services on Sunday. He's made friends there and really enjoys it.

Unfortunately, he will be singing on Christmas Eve and Christmas morning, so our tradition of going out as a threesome to the mall, then Disneyland will be down to two. And Christmas morning will not consist of Dale asking when our son will ever get out of bed to open gifts.

I'm wondering if we'll even leave the holiday lights on all night to help Santa find our house. If we have holiday lights, that is.

The second change is that Dale is currently in Massachusetts on business. He won't be back until December 20th. This means I will be decorating and getting the tree and doing all the things as a solo that I usually do with my husband as a couple.

I used to do all the decorating myself, when I was a single gal, including the tree. Of course, I never got a tree over five feet tall, because I couldn't carry one bigger than that. I'm not sure how that's going to look in our living room with its vaulted ceiling.

Perhaps I could set it on a table.

I may need to, anyway. I'm not certain how the new dog will handle having a live tree in the house. Yes, we still have Spazz, although we have christened her Lady Spazzleton to give her a little dignity. I still call her Spazz, but Dale calls her Lady. I'm not sure who's more confused at this point, me or her.

She is a female, so I don't have to worry about leg lifting, but she is a notorious chewer. So far, I've lost three leashes, her car harness, a seatbelt (that one was expensive), and half of the fringe from my Oriental carpet. On the plus side, it's easier to clean now that the fringe doesn't get sucked into the vacuum.

She and Duffy enjoy bringing sticks and branches inside from the backyard so they can chew them to splinters on my carpet. I fear what they might think when they see an entire tree come into the house.

Even if she doesn't try to eat the tree, she and Duffy have wrestling matches that surpass anything on TV. Sometimes this results in fallen furniture. I usually tie the tree to the wall to keep it from toppling over, but this year, I may have to build a fence around it, too.

Perhaps this year Dale and I will enjoy a Christmas Eve of Disneyland magic, followed by picking the tree up off the floor and trying to salvage a few ornaments. On Christmas morning we can share a walk with the dogs while we wait for Marcus. I'm not worried about our traditions.

The Carlines can adapt.

KEEPING THE HOME FIRES BURNING

Over the twenty-plus years Dale and I have been together, we have both had our share of business travel. While I worked at Raytheon, we each took turns traveling to different military bases and demonstrating equipment. Our bosses were kind enough to not schedule these visits together, so that one of us could be at home with Marcus. Most trips were about a week in length.

In marital terms, this is just long enough to get used to not cooking dinner, but not long enough to change the presets on the car radio.

Apart from missing my husband, leaving Marcus when he was a baby was the hardest part of my travel. Of course I didn't have to worry about anything. Dale was an excellent parent and I knew he'd take good care of our son.

As long as I didn't know that they were eating Oreos

for dinner every night, it was all good.

I remember one trip in particular, when Marcus was seven. One of the songs I used to sing to him at bedtime was the Beatles' *All My Loving*. While I drove Marcus to school that morning, I told him that I was going to be gone a few days, but not to worry. Dad would take care of him. Marcus responded to my explanation by telling me about the latest Pokémon move he had learned and how many points he had.

Our conversation was not even in the same zip code, let alone the same vehicle.

I surrendered to the possibility that my son did not care that I would be gone. "Don't miss me too much," I snarked.

Suddenly I heard something from the back seat. Marcus was singing.

"Close your eyes and I'll kiss you. Tomorrow I'll miss you…" He sang the entire song to me before he got out of the minivan.

They may have had to shove me onto the plane at that point, because I really didn't want to go.

Those days are gone. With Marcus in Long Beach, he is unaware of my travel plans unless I text him. Now I only travel for horse shows and author events. Even Dale's business trips have been few and far between, until recently.

Dale was sent to Massachusetts on company business for a month. Not just any month, but December. This means I will be doing all the decorating. I may also be doing a little more shopping. Dale usually shops for his family, but if he's not around I may have to help him out.

I already do all the holiday baking, but this year, there will not be any men in my house to eat the cookies and fudge. If I bake now, there will be more for me to eat and I'll have to ask Santa if I can borrow his suit after the holidays. Nothing else will fit me.

And as for holiday concerts, events, and parties, prepare to see me as a party of one.

I could complain about the company sending him so far away for an entire month during the holiday season, but I can't. Every time I try, I think of people who have loved ones in the military. I have friends who served several tours in Vietnam. Their wives took care of the house, the kids, and basically everything while they were gone. When I asked one them how they did it, one of my friends just shrugged and said, "You did what needed to be done."

If they never whined about it, how can I kvetch?

SCALING BACK WHILE LOOKING BACK

When I was growing up, my family made Christmas a huge deal. There were decorations everywhere, an avalanche of cookies, and a mountain of presents.

Is it any wonder the rest of the year paled in comparison?

Of course, the decorations were mostly handmade, as were the cookies. As for all those presents, they were lots of little things wrapped up, from pairs of socks to sets of jacks.

As an adult, I was driven to continue my family's traditions. Even as a single gal, I made the most out of the season with decorations, baking, and gifts.

When Dale and I married and had Marcus, the holiday reached rather epic proportions. Decorating a two-bedroom condo was easy. Putting up lights and garlands in a four-bedroom house was not. I may not have done any more baking, but it got a little harder once there was a toddler helping me. And let's just say the presents took over the living room.

Over the years, Dale and Marcus have been trying to train me to downsize everything I do for Christmas. I have gone from baking several dozen cookies, to only making one batch of sugar cookies and one batch of fudge. And they have both shown me the simplicity of a couple of desired gifts, instead of an excess of doo-dads.

But they haven't found a way to keep me from hanging lights and tinsel everywhere. I've decorated this way forever. Nothing could keep me from putting up the ornaments and angels.

Until this year.

With Dale out of town and Marcus in Long Beach, the boxes of decorations sat in our living room for a week, waiting for me. I kept putting them off. First it was because the house needed to be tidier. Then it was because I still didn't have the tree. Finally I realized why nothing had been decorated.

All the changes with my family this Christmas had de-motivated me.

Finally I decided to try. I cleaned up the house and opened the bins. The Nativity scene came out, followed by the wreaths for the front door, then the hanger for the Christmas cards that will soon arrive. Slowly, over the course of two days, everything in the boxes came out.

I still don't have a tree yet, but that's next.

Unfortunately, my decorating spree activated my need to bake. Each day I remind myself that cookies will not be good for my diet, and each day I check the fridge to see how much butter I have, in case I want to make just one batch.

It also awakened my nostalgia muscle. I wanted to return to that time when Marcus was little and do all the things we used to do. This included visiting Santa, seeing the Christmas parade at Disneyland, and going to the toy store with Dale to buy our son's gifts.

Even if he was not busy with final exams, I doubt if I could get my twenty-year old son to sit on Santa's lap, he doesn't have time for parades, and I'm pretty certain he does not want any Legos, Brio, or Hot Wheels cars.

I can purchase a few toys to donate to other children, but the Santa trip will have to remain a memory. I can't think of any parent who'd let me rent their child for that outing.

So I'll rein in my impulses to fill the living room with gifts and the kitchen with delights. But don't judge me if a Hot Wheels car finds its way into Marcus's stocking.

I could have done more.

GETTING HELP WHILE I CAN

I thought I knew what I was going to talk about this week: getting the Christmas tree. With Dale gone and Marcus up to his ears in final exams, I was going to have to pick out a tree, get it home, and get it into our house by myself. I had visions that involved creativity, contorted body positions, and lots of pain relievers.

It was a perfect subject for a column.

When I was single, I always got my own tree. Of course that was over twenty years ago. The only year I struggled was the time I misjudged the size and bought a seven foot pine with a fat trunk. It was also the year I lived in an apartment on the second floor.

It took me almost an hour to drag that puppy up two flights of stairs.

This year, I decided to take baby steps. First, I would

take my time at the choose-and-cut lot, and pick out a tree that I could manage. Next, I would choose a day to pick it up. Last, I'd figure out how to get it into the house.

The idea began to unravel immediately. Between all of my other activities, I managed to carve out half-an-hour to shop leisurely for a tree. I tried not to feel rushed as I wandered through the lot, looking for something suitable.

As I walked, I told myself, "Five foot tree, five foot tree, well, no more than six feet, hey, look at that tall one. It's perfect."

It was at least seven feet tall. I grabbed the trunk. It was fairly small. I jiggled it back and forth. It felt light. We live in a one-story house. I could do this.

It would be easy to roll the tree from the top of the minivan onto the driveway. I just had to keep the branches from breaking upon impact.

I thought, briefly, about dragging one of the mattresses outside to absorb the blow.

God must have seen my impending disaster, and pointed me to Marcus's Facebook status. He claimed to have gotten through the most exhausting part of his month and could now relax. I contacted my son and asked if he could spare half an hour helping me with the tree.

He could, especially if it was followed by lunch.

I'd like to tell you some hilarious tale about me and my son, trying to get a skinny tree into a fat tree stand and keep the dogs from pulling it over. The truth is, I don't think the Carlines have ever gotten a Christmas tree erected so quickly and easily. It was a world record.

There was no story to tell, only a lunch date to enjoy.

We had a nice conversation at the restaurant, about all kinds of things. One subject was Marcus's school plans. He explained that after Long Beach, he thought he'd do his post-graduate work out of state. It turns out Texas and Miami both have excellent music schools, although he'd like to relocate to Vancouver, if he could find a school there.

It suddenly dawned on me that my son would be truly leaving someday, and someday was coming sooner than I thought. My Do-It-Yourself holiday had turned into a reality-slap Christmas.

So my story about getting a tree is really about facing facts. I had to admit I needed help with the tree, just as I have to admit I'll be sad when my son is no longer around. In the meantime, I'll enjoy our time together, and admire our handiwork.

The tree looks great.

THE GIFT THAT KEEPS ON GIVING... HEADACHES

Now that the holidays are officially over, it's time to deal with the aftermath. In addition to taking down decorations and disposing of another dead pine tree, there are gifts to be put away.

We are eternally grateful for what we receive, but we wish we knew where to put it.

I know many of you have already done all these things. This is because you don't live with my husband, who insists that the decorations stay up until after his birthday, which is January 2nd.

He also believes there is a fairy godmaid who gathers all the empty boxes and gift bags so they can be either recycled for next year or retired to the trash. So let's just say our home lags behind everyone else by about a week.

My gifts this year were fairly easy to store. I got some

DVDs, a gift card, and a Swiss Army knife, which I needed badly, since I lost my old one. Marcus' gifts all traveled with him to his apartment in Long Beach, so I don't have to worry about their clutter unless he moves back to our house. Knowing the chances of that, perhaps I should say "until."

Dale's gifts are equally storable, with one exception. One of his brothers got him a stadium blanket, also known as a throw. I am a big fan of throws and have several around the house. They are great to wrap around my lap on cool evenings, and usually can be tossed in the washer and dryer without harm.

The new throw is purple and gold flannel, with the Lakers Basketball logo all over it. There are lots of sports-themed throws that are nice looking. This is not one of them. I'd like to use the term "garish" in the best possible way here. The purple and gold are so loud, you almost need sunglasses to look at it. It is also edged in fat strips of flannel fringe, which gives the whole thing a puffy, almost feminine look.

Dale loved it anyway.

"We can put this on top of our bedspread," he told me when he opened it.

I tried to answer, but I could only get a few guttural noises out as I searched for a tactful way to say, "Not if you ever want me to actually sleep in our bed again." I'm pretty sure the colors would keep me awake all night.

Still gurgling and stuttering, I turned to Marcus, who was laughing.

"This is going to become just like the leg lamp in A Christmas Story," he said.

I began to picture the eternal struggle between Dale and me. He would spread the throw across our bed and I would come up with some excuse why it had to be somewhere else. It would probably need washing frequently, as either something would accidentally be spilled on it, or the cat would have some kind of mishap.

While being washed and dried, I would silently pray it would behave like an errant sock and disappear.

If I couldn't keep it in the washer or dryer, perhaps I could be helpful and move it to a safe location to keep it away from the cat or the dogs or terrorists or something. After all, I must protect anything my husband loves so much.

As it turns out, we compromised. The throw is now on the chair at the end of the bed, where Dale sits and watches sports, including his beloved Lakers. I don't have to look at it.

Now if I could just get those decorations put away.

PREPARING FOR HOLIDAYS REQUIRES PREP WORK

How did the holidays get here so soon? One minute I was packing for our summer vacation, and the next thing I know, I'm unpacking reindeer for the lawn.

Now that Halloween is over, my already-full schedule has some additional tasks to be squeezed in. I have to call Mario to trim the trees so Dale can hang the lights. I have to start bugging my family for ideas about Christmas gifts.

I also need to make Dale find out whether we are hosting Christmas this year for his family. For years, all the Carlines traveled to the outer reaches of Norwalk to celebrate the day at my mother-in-law's home. A few years ago, we all seemed to wake up to the fact that she did most of the preparation and cooking and was probably exhausted by the merriment.

Mom deserved a break.

121

So Dale and his three brothers decided that Christmas would rotate around our houses. Older brother Dennis got a waiver, since he and Debbie live in Oregon. It's hard to get three other families that far from home for the holidays, no matter how much fun it would be to spend time with them.

I think David and Pam hosted the first year, then Dale and I had everyone over at our home. In theory, the next year was supposed to go to youngest brother Daryl and Tanya.

I might point out here that they live in Lancaster. Granted, it's not Oregon, but it's also not the place you want to think about driving home from after a day of festivities and too much turkey and stuffing.

So last year, David and Pam entertained the family again. Being a former software engineer, I naturally used my scientific sense of logic to arrive at a hypothesis: It should be our turn again.

"Are we hosting Christmas this year?" I asked Dale.

He looked confused. "Who did it last year?"

This is the obvious answer for most men, who enjoy a carefree day of being with their families and don't stress about the pre-Christmas cleaning or cooking. And even though I know that Dale's family is my family, there are different levels of cleaning depending upon who is visiting.

Dale's family requires several weeks of hard scrubbing, if only because I love them too much to subject them to the massive amounts of hair left by two dogs. I can clean the carpets, but I may have to burn the furniture.

This is why I need to know now about my hosting duties. Amazon may not offer one-day free shipping if I have to order a flamethrower.

Last time, I scoured, mopped, vacuumed and otherwise sterilized every surface in our house, including washing all the drapes. My sister-in-law still got a stuffy nose from her cat allergies.

In addition, my nephews wanted to play with Duffy, but weren't certain how to do it, so I spent most of the time keeping him from chasing them and barking, which made them run, screaming with fright.

It wasn't as much fun as it sounds.

This year, we have the added delight of Lady Spazzleton, our retriever, who I'm sure will join in the chase. If the boys weren't terrified before, they will now forever remember our house as the place of nightmares.

I've marked the calendar with due dates for all of these tasks, leaving room for shopping, wrapping, and parties. There's only one thing left for me to schedule.

I'll need at least one day to panic.

PICTURING THE PERFECT GROUP SHOT

Most people have heard of the Carline Christmas Photo Extravaganza, where I drag Dale, Marcus, the dogs and the cat out to the ranch in Chino Hills and take pictures with our horses for the annual card.

It took us years to learn how to organize everyone so we could get the picture taken before sunset. Now all we have to do is smile for the camera while we keep the animals from mauling each other and us.

Sometimes I think I should sell tickets.

And yet nothing quite compares to the annual holiday photo of the Placentia Library staff and trustees. I got to do this last year for the first time, and it was great fun. This year was no different. There were no animals involved, but getting so many people together is always a challenge.

We were hoping to take the picture in our newly

remodeled and remarkable community meeting room. The Placentia Library Friends Foundation kicked in the lion's share of money to upgrade the space from floor to ceiling and everything in between. If you haven't seen it, it's now seriously gorgeous.

It's also very popular, so it was unavailable for a photo shoot.

The staff and trustees gathered in the back corner of the library instead, where we took the picture last year. Previously, we all wore red or green sweaters, along with Santa hats. This year was a southern California holiday—we were in beachwear.

This year was also different in that we had to take the photo during business hours, which meant we kept losing staff members who had to run off and help customers. I admit, customers do trump posing in sunglasses and a Hawaiian shirt.

Jeanette Contreras, our intrepid library director, really likes to direct. She knows that a group picture cannot be thrown together. There is a certain balance to be achieved, so she made certain we were all sitting, standing, or otherwise filling the spaces to make the best shot possible.

I sat down next to our newest trustee, Jo-Anne Martin, and made jokes with her while Jeanette arranged, then rearranged everyone's position around us. Every once in a while, I would catch my voice getting a little too loud to be in a library. I kept waiting for one of the staff to turn around and shush me.

No one was paying attention, probably because they were too busy running between the customers and their position for the photo.

As usual, Al Shkoler was our photographer. After Jeanette had worked her magic, he shuffled a few more folks around to get everyone in the shot, and to keep the palm trees from looking like they were growing out of people's heads.

We had a few false starts with the camera. First, the timer went off too soon. Then it didn't go off at all. Then the flash didn't work. Then it did. All through it, everyone was patient and smiled on cue, no matter what happened.

At last, we got several pictures taken. The best one of the bunch showed an exuberant group of people wishing everyone a joyous holiday.

I can't wait to see our photo on the library's holiday cards. Getting a good picture of a large group may or may not be harder than a smaller group, but at least no one was trying to maul anyone.

SAYING YES TO THE HOLIDAYS

Christmas seems early this year, and I don't know about you, but it feels like I'm squeezing every last second out of every minute these days to get things done. All of our holiday events are running at warp speed, so my calendar is listing several activities each day.

I suppose I could learn to say "no" but where's the fun in that?

Last Wednesday morning, I was at the Placentia Round Table for the monthly gathering of the Women's Club. I've been invited to speak there next month, and Nancy Melton, Vice President of Programs, asked me to come as her guest in order to meet the members and get an idea of what the club is about.

This was not my first invitation to the Women's Club. Quite a few of my library friends have invited me, including

Brenda Benner and Nancy Tollefson. Even Judi Carmona has asked me to attend. Until now, I've had to say no. Since my column deadline is Wednesday morning, I'm afraid to commit to any events that might tear me away from any last-minute editing.

Still, somehow I managed to pull everything together and attend this meeting during the one month I was already spinning out of control.

It was a fun event. I saw many familiar faces and met many new ones. I also learned this is a dangerous organization for me. Their mission is to raise money and supplies to donate to others in our community. This means a lot of women volunteering for a lot of activities.

Everyone knows what a sucker I am for volunteer duties. At the luncheon, they were asking for people to help out. I kept wanting to raise my hand, and I'm not even a member.

I'm definitely going to enjoy my visit with these ladies in January. My New Year's resolutions may have to include writing down all my current responsibilities before I sign up for anything.

You'd think that one holiday event a day would be enough, but the Placentia Tamale Festival was being held the same evening. Yes, I'd already spent three hours with some delightful women, then worked at the ranch. I should have gone home and relaxed after such a full day.

But I had a dream to fulfill.

I've been to the Tamale Festival quite a few times, and each time I've gotten there, I've been too late. Everyone was out of tamales. This year, I was on a mission. I was going to the Tamale Festival and eat a tamale.

"We need to go to the festival," I told Dale. "I'll be

128

home at 5:30."

In Dale-hours, this translated to 6 p.m. which was still acceptable. We drove over to Old Town Placentia and walked up and down the street, admiring all the bright lights and bustle of the crowds. Music was blasting everywhere. There were lots of people and food and drink in a small space, but everyone was happy and polite and having a good time.

After wandering back and forth, I finally settled on the booth outside Tlaquepaque and got a chicken tamale plate. We found an empty table near the bridge and watched the trains go by. The evening was wonderful and the tamale was delicious. I returned home with a full stomach and warm heart.

So I was treated to great company and great traditions twice in one day. All I had to do was believe I was too busy.

TWINKLING THROUGH THE SEASON

I have loved the Christmas season for as long as I can remember. It was never about the presents, or the time off from school and work. It was always about the decorations. I'm a sucker for twinkling lights and the smell of evergreen trees. I love red ribbons and shiny ornaments.

And don't get me started on angels.

When I was a child, my parents would take me and my brother for car rides to look at the lights on people's houses. In those days, outdoor lights were all huge colored bulbs. No one had faux-icicles hanging from their eaves or animated deer in their yards.

I loved the homes that were outlined in lights, and when the bulbs were all the same color, my love was elevated to adoration. Someday, I vowed, I would have an elegant house like these.

Then I married Dale, whose motto for outside Christmas lights is, the more the merrier. I don't mind. He's proud of his outdoor creations and they're very twinkly, so I'm happy.

Indoor decorating always revolves around the tree. When I am a guest in someone's home, I love to see what kind of tree they have and how they've decorated it. Is it a real tree or an artificial one? Are their ornaments color-coordinated?

I remember, one of my mother's friends had a fabulous tree. It was a real tree, decorated with those large lights that bubbled like mini-lava lamps. The ornaments had an antique feel to them. Of course, at my advancing age, now they are antique. In particular, there was a Santa, a sleigh, and eight reindeer, all stretched across the branches.

It was easy for a small child like me to get lost in that miniature world.

Our tree was always a mishmash of ornaments and lights. We lived in a small house with low ceilings, so each Christmas tree lives in my memory as round and squatty. My brother and I decorated it, so it usually looked like it was exploding with bells and balls and tinsel.

Apart from having a chopped-down tree in the living room, no one decorated the rest of their house for the holiday, as far as I know. We didn't even hang up our stockings, since we didn't have a fireplace. Santa brought them each year, already filled.

I'm not sure how he got our stockings. It just happened, and when you're a child who wants to believe in Santa Claus, you don't ask questions.

At some point in my adulthood, I began decorating all my rooms with some little reminder of the season. Festive towels went in the bathroom. Lighted garlands went over the windows. Any place that could hold a twinkly light or an angel figurine was anointed.

When I lived in my condo, this took me one joyous day. I continued the one day decorating tradition when we moved into our house, but over the years, I've realized it's a marathon to get everything done in such a short time.

This year, I've been throwing tinsel around my house for a week and I'm still not finished. Perhaps I'm getting older, but I refuse to believe that. I keep telling myself that I'm learning to enjoy the journey.

I hope the journey ends before I have to host Christmas dinner. In the meantime, as long as there are some twinkling lights for me to look at, I'm happy.

I CELEBRATE MANY WONDERFUL LIVES

We have many traditions at this time of year, including holiday movies. From all the versions of Ebenezer Scrooge, to films about Santa Claus, they are designed to tug at our hearts, and make us reflect on our lives.

The most recognized is probably *It's a Wonderful Life*. Clarence, the almost-angel, shows poor, desperate George Bailey what the world would look like if he'd never been born. By the end of the film, the entire town is pouring into the Bailey household to save George, declaring him "the richest man in town."

I've seen it at least once a year for all my adulthood and I'm still a puddle of sentimental tears by the time the credits roll.

The movie's goal is to make us look at our own lives and see how we have affected those around us. Unlike the main character, I don't know if I've truly shaped the world around me. I never saved my brother's life, or kept a town going financially.

Although I've supplied moments of entertainment for some (and flashes of frustration for others) my own wonderful life has been worth it mostly to supply the world with my delightful son, who I suspect will do bigger and better things than I ever could.

But I know I've been influenced by others. Yes, I have my family, who keep my soul contented. And there are my friends. They help me get a little crazy, laugh a little too loud and get a little too cheeky.

There are others, though, who don't quite fit on those lists. They're possibly acquaintances, or even strangers, and they put the icing on top of each day for me.

First are the people in the groups I belong to, from the Placentia Library to my local chapter of Sisters in Crime. Inside my fun-loving nature still lives the shy girl I used to be, and sometimes when I walk into a crowded room, I want to slink along a wall and sit where no one can notice me.

Until someone greets me with a smile, and even a hug. When I see that face, so glad to see mine, my shyness melts. Not only do I know I'm where I belong, it gives me the confidence to greet others with the same cheer I've received. Good spirits and inclusion are contagious.

Second are the people I meet when I'm buying my groceries, doing some shopping, or having a meal out. Recently I was at an electronics store, looking for one of Dale's presents. The clerk was a personable young man. He acted happy to explain everything to me, plus share a little of his personal life.

Was he doing his job as a salesman? Yes, and there's

nothing wrong with that. We talked about our families, laughed, and I walked out with exactly what I wanted.

After, I went to the grocery store where my favorite checkout clerk smiled and asked how my holidays were going. We discussed recipes and the sweet relaxation we feel when the meal is over and last dish is washed.

Could I have gotten through my day without these folks? Yes. Would it have been as much fun? I don't know. All I can say is that my day was richer for crossing their paths.

Like George Bailey, I'm really having a wonderful life. Unlike him, I don't need an angel to tell me. I'm thankful for it every day.

Holiday Baking Isn't for Cowards

There's nothing like the holidays to bring out the baker in me. Let me be clear. I am not one of those bakers who can toss things together and make culinary magic. I'm the kind of baker with an extensive array of cookbooks.

Recipes are my friends. I can follow a darned good recipe to make darned good cookies. If the cookies don't turn out, it's got to be the recipe's fault.

In my youth, I used to make cookies as gifts. They were more work than purchasing something, but definitely cheaper. I remember spending days in the teeny kitchen in my condo with parchment paper on every flat surface, covered with everything from sugar cookies to Mexican wedding cookies.

The air was always thick with flour and confectioner's sugar.

136

I like to make cakes, too, but they are problematic. Even when Marcus was around the house, there weren't enough people to eat a whole cake, not even if we each had a slice every night for a week.

I'm not a child of the Depression, but I was raised by people who did live through it, and I can't stand to see anything go to waste, even if it means it ends up going to my waist.

Pies are better, in terms of being able to make them and watch them disappear. Each Thanksgiving, I must prepare a pumpkin pie for dinner with our friends, as it's the only pie their son will eat. I don't quite understand this, because I not only follow a recipe, it's the recipe on the can of pumpkin I buy at the store.

And here's a shocker: I use those pre-made, rolled up crusts from the dairy section.

Sadly, I've never perfected the pie crust. It's not the recipe's fault, unless all of them are bad. I've tried recipes from Betty Crocker to James Beard and they all end up the texture of cardboard. I'm pretty sure I overwork the dough each time, but I can't leave it alone.

Anything worth doing is worth doing to excess, right?

My grandmother used to make this fabulous pie crust, where she would substitute strawberry soda for the ice water. Not only was the crust flaky, but the soda gave the layers a crisp, sugary taste that enhanced the filling. I've tried to recreate this more than once. Each attempt ended badly.

I sure wish I'd paid more attention when she was baking. That woman had mad skills.

This year I am again attempting the impossible (for me) homemade pie crust. As much as I love reading cookbooks, I am equally hooked on certain cooking shows. I recently watched one of my favorite TV women bake a caramel apple pie. It looked so delicious, I could almost smell it from the screen.

Her website had the recipe, plus a pictorial step-by-step, plus a video. With all that help, I am bound to succeed this time, right?

Wish me luck. If it all goes well, I'll serve it at dinner tomorrow. If the pie crust is a bust, I have the pre-made crust standing by. If the pie doesn't work out, I'll serve the apple filling over ice cream. If that doesn't work, I'll toss it all in the trash and tell no one.

Not only do I have a Plan B, I have Plans A through D. I'll let you all know which plan got served for dessert.

DECKING THE HALLS WITH HOLIDAY SPIRIT

The Christmas season is my favorite time of the year. I love the twinkling lights, the smell of spices and evergreens, and even the cheerful, cheesy holiday songs. The only thing I don't love is all the work it takes to get my house in that shape.

I used to spend an entire day decorating my home for the season. Every room got some dash of holiday cheer. By the time the sun had set, it looked like Christmas had not only invaded my house, it had taken prisoners.

When I got married, I roped Dale into the festivities. He hangs the lights on the outside. I'm pretty sure he'd like to put together a holiday extravaganza like the houses that end up on YouTube.

The only thing stopping him is the size of the loan we'd have to take out to make that happen.

I've tried for many years to get him and Marcus

engaged in the centerpiece of my decorating—the tree. When Marcus was little, I had this dream of a wonderful family day spent picking out a tree, bringing it home, and decorating it together.

Dale's dream was a little different. He pictured wandering around with me while I chose the tree, then putting it in the stand for me to decorate. That's where his dream ended. His creative side is limited to the outdoor lights.

I'm not sure what Marcus' dream was during all this, but he seemed happier once we were back home and he could return to the comfort of his room. His room with the small, artificial tree.

A couple of Christmases ago, I started to think about having to un-decorate the house as I went from room to room hanging tinsel. I'd never thought about it before. Dale likes the house to stay decorated until his birthday on January 2nd. I've always spent the next day tearing everything down and putting it away.

Now I was thinking about how much work that was. This resulted in my hesitance to put something in every room, something that I'd pull down a few weeks later. Coincidentally, this was the year I accidentally bought a short Christmas tree. We have a vaulted ceiling in the living room, but at 5'2", everything looks tall to me.

The tree I brought home could not hold all our ornaments. I carefully chose the ones I liked the best, and found that, the following year, those were the only ornaments I wanted to put on.

I admit, I worried about not putting everything out. Was I losing my Christmas spirit? Would I become a curmudgeon that puts a plastic tree on the dining room table and calls it quits?

This year, I've put out what I love and left the rest in their boxes, all without remorse. My Christmas spirit has taken a turn, away from my self-imposed decorating duties and toward enjoying the season. The time I spent hanging garlands is better used to do things for others. I can pull out clothes to donate, purchase a toy for a tot, and of course, help my library.

And if one day I have a single, tiny tree on my table, it won't make me a curmudgeon. It means I'd rather demonstrate my Christmas spirit, and not just show it off.

WHEN CHRISTMAS TRADITIONS ARE WORTH THE WORK

Parents naturally pass traditions down the family branches, and our family is no different. Friendships are part of that tradition. My parents had many friends, just as Dale and I have. Not only has Marcus watched us have our own lives, he is friends with our friends' children.

Christmas, especially, was a time of sending cards to everyone my parents knew. It was a laborious process, and done by my mother. Each card was signed, then addressed, stamped and sent off with my father to be mailed.

My mother didn't have a driver's license, or she would have done that, too.

Like her, I am in charge of Christmas cards at our house. We also have many friends, perhaps more than my folks had. Unlike my mom, I have technology on my side.

The year I realized I was writing the same news in all my cards, I knew it was time to write a Christmas letter. The first one was brief but memorable—Dale's cousin Amanda told me, "I loved your Christmas letter. I hope you're writing more than that."

Thus began my second career.

Along with the letter, we started our tradition of taking a family picture. We began with a simple pose by the fireplace, then included the pets, then went to the ranch to get the horses involved.

It's now almost a science. Dale and Marcus wrangle the dogs and cat while I get the horses out of their stalls. We get everyone posed, sort of, and my horse trainer takes multiple pictures with our digital camera.

The trick is for the humans to keep smiling while we keep the dogs sitting, and my black horse from licking the cat. It takes about a week for the cat to forgive us.

I still try to keep the letter short. It's one page of the Carlines' highs and lows for the year, plus some kind of musing on making the world a better place. I send everything to an online card service, print my own labels, then spend an evening stuffing envelopes.

Over the years, I thought my list would dwindle, but it keeps growing instead. I now send out nearly 100 cards every year.

Sadly, I remember when my mother stopped sending cards. For a few years, she culled her list, saying she was only going to send cards to people who sent them to her. Then she made more cuts, to people she saw regularly. Why send them cards when she saw them often?

It probably took five years for her to stop sending any cards at all.

The worst part of this story is when I watched my parents lose all contact with the friends I had grown up knowing. Sometimes I wonder if they missed these people, and whether they began to slip apart the moment they stopped sending cards at Christmas.

I love giving the cards as much as I love receiving them from people. I don't get a card from everyone on my list, but I don't care. In my opinion, it's better to keep sending out a sign of life each year. Who knows when our glad tidings is the boost a lonely friend needs?

And I still send cards to the people I see all the time. It's like a little holiday gift we give each other. I'm not letting these folks slip away from me, especially not at Christmas.

CHRISTMAS PHOTOS THRU THE YEARS

Our first, professional attempt

Frostie's (the horse) first year, joining Katy the cat and
Mikey the Corgi.

Snoopy has joined us, and we have a new dog, Duffy

Our latest year. Lady Spazzleton has joined Duffy, giving us a 2-dog household.

HAPPY NEW YEAR!

Resolutions, Big and Small

It's the first week of January—do you know where your resolutions are? Of course you do. They've met with my resolutions and are all thumbing a ride to Neverland, since they will never be kept.

I guess we try to make New Year's resolutions because we want to start off the new year with a clean slate and a new attitude. At the ripe old age of none-of-your-business, I've decided that my slate doesn't need cleaning and there's nothing wrong with my attitude. It took me years to get here, but I have finally resolved to give up making New Year's resolutions.

As a child, I took the whole thing very seriously and made very somber vows about keeping my room clean and doing what my mom asked the first time she asked me. These pledges lasted until about noon on January 2nd, when I decided to watch one more cartoon before hanging my coat up as Mom requested. I spent about half a minute in guilt over my broken promise, then scampered off to do something fun.

Adulthood meant more adult resolutions. I joined the millions who resolve to go to the gym, lose weight, remember birthdays, and get a better life. I'm pretty sure that none of these common, if heartfelt, resolutions made it very far into the new year. They all dropped away, one by one, as I blew off the gym in favor of going to a movie, and worked so much overtime that I forgot to mail anyone their birthday cards.

In my early thirties, I decided that these kinds of resolutions only led to guilt and disappointment, so I began a tradition of making only resolutions that I knew I could keep. For example, I thought of the worst movie I had seen that year and resolved never to see it again. I resolved not to feed potato skins to the garbage disposal, since I knew they clogged the pipes. On the positive side, I resolved to take my dog for walks, because I lived in a Placentia Lakes condo and didn't have a backyard. Now that I live in a house with a yard, that resolution had to be tossed. This nifty little New Year's scheme kept me in worry-free promises for many years, before I finally acknowledged that it was silly and meaningless and gave it up.

These days, I've decided that each day is the beginning of a new year of days. Some days I resolve to do certain things or stop doing other things, and some days I succeed. As for the rest of the days, I just muddle through them, trying to get from Point A to Point B in my life without wrecking anything in between.

But if pressed for a New Year's resolution, I can always pull out the old standby, and pledge never to watch a movie I hated again. All I can say is, thank God for RoboCop.

HELPING OTHERS HELP THEMSELVES

Even though I try to resist the temptation to make New Year's resolutions, I do feel a general need each year to "make some changes." I spend every January in a flurry of activity. The house is cleaned, files are organized, and I'm on a diet and exercise regimen.

By February, the floors are no longer being swept daily. I start piling mail on the dining room table again in March. Healthy eating succumbs to the dreaded chocolate Easter bunny, and the dog and I decide not to go out for walks because it's too hot or too cold or too windy or too boring.

When I think about it, I'm actually not making any changes at all. I'm just completing tasks that I'm already supposed to be doing.

What I'd really like to do is set goals for everyone else. People pay for personal shoppers and life coaches, so there's obviously a market for letting other people tell you what to do. Why not hire someone to create your New Year's resolutions? I could offer a range of ideas, from mild, like changing your hairstyle, to life-altering, like changing your hair stylist.

Take my own family, for example.

Dale is having problems with his knee. He's always been very athletic, and has never met a sport that he hasn't injured himself playing. Icing his knees is a normal part of his life. But this newest pain is, in his words, "like nothing I've ever felt before." He is trying every home remedy in his arsenal. Heat, ice, elevating the leg, stretching the leg, over-the-counter pain relievers, nothing is working.

My resolution for him would be to go see the doctor. If I had a New Year's resolutions business, I could actually earn money for this simple suggestion.

Marcus, on the other hand, needs a package deal.

Let's start with the t-shirts. He has many shirts that he loves, despite the fact that they are mere ribbons of cotton, strung together by a frayed neckband. One of his shirts is a St. Patrick's Day novelty he got in sixth grade. In addition to being holey, it continues to climb up his torso as he grows. Yet, he cannot part with it, or any of these relics. He even asks for them when I've done the laundry. With a closet full of new shirts, he will still ask, "Mom, where's my Irish shirt," as though it's the only one worth wearing.

And then, there's his practice of leaving things where he last touched them. We have hair picks scattered in every room, as well as both cars, because he drops them as soon as his hair is done. If he comes out of his room to share a song with me on the guitar, the instrument is left on the couch. Shoes are in the family room, the peanut butter is on the

152

kitchen table, and it's a good day when his backpack is not blocking a doorway.

I could make a year's salary with his resolutions.

Seriously, I doubt if anyone would want to pay for that kind of service. We can tell ourselves we need to lose a few pounds. Why would you pay for that suggestion? Maybe I'll just stick to giving myself advice, and hope that someday I take it.

And next year, when January 1st rolls around and I feel like making some changes, I resolve to go lie down until the feeling passes.

CHANGING A COUPLE OF THINGS

It's January 1st, and you know what that means. It's time to make our New Year's resolutions. I've made lots of resolutions over the years, from the serious to the silly. Every year, I tell myself not to make these stupid promises, and every year, I think of a few things I'd like to do differently in the next twelve months.

Some of my resolutions have to do with my everyday life. For example, yesterday morning, I resolved to wait until the dishwasher had completed all of its cycles before getting into the shower. It's a simple promise, one I should have made long ago, but yesterday's sudden burst of cold water down my back reminded me. It's just one of those promises you find yourself making more than once a year, like, vowing every day to put your shoes away, only after you've tripped over them.

I also resolve to find a way to remember to take my eco-friendly bags into the grocery store with me. In an attempt to reduce my carbon footprint, I bought four green bags to take my groceries home in. Unfortunately, even though I keep them in my minivan, I can't seem to remember to take them into the store. I'm always halfway through my shopping before I remember. I do find ways to recycle the plastic bags, but it kind of defeats the purpose.

Other resolutions are for more sporadic events. I've already resolved to make my yearly mammogram actually occur every year. It's an entry on my computer's calendar, waiting to alert me. But there are other yearly promises to make.

Let's start with our taxes. Every year, I wander through the house, digging for receipts and statements, and arrive at our accountant's office thinking I've got everything he needs. And every year, I've missed something. This year, I'd like to get through the tax appointment without having him sigh quietly and raise his eyebrows. So I resolve to get better at finding those pieces of paper.

For Halloween, I resolve to buy one bag of candy next year. In truth, I wanted to buy one bag of candy this year; last year, we didn't have a lot of trick-or-treaters. Dale was concerned that we didn't have enough candy and told me to buy two more. Next year, I resolve to remind him that we had two unopened bags of candy at the end of the night. Two bags that we didn't need to eat, but did.

Of course, I always promise to start our holiday shopping early, and to set aside time for baking, decorating and entertaining. Sometimes I meet this resolution, and sometimes I'm racing down to the wire, completely stressed. I've decided not to make any changes to the way I get things done for Christmas. The Internet has made my shopping easy, and everything else gets completed, eventually.

I do resolve, however, to add two events to my holiday season. One is the Placentia Library's presentation of "A Child's Christmas in Wales". I volunteered at the library for the evening and was delighted by the songs and poetry. Next year, I plan to take my family. The second is the Maverick Theater's play, "Santa Claus Conquers the Martians". Dale, Marcus, and I went to see it and didn't stop laughing from the moment it started, to the curtain call.

I'm not certain how many of these resolutions I'll keep, but if nothing else works, I at least resolve to have as much fun as possible in 2009. That should be a promise I can keep.

GHOSTS OF RESOLUTIONS PAST

I'd like a show of hands: who made New Year's resolutions this year? Now that we're 5 days into 2012, who has already broken at least one of their resolutions?

Wow, so many of you.

Over the years, I've had my share of resolutions. I can never decide whether to make them or not. In reality, I know how silly they are. For example, I've resolved to lose weight and get in shape more years than I can count. Yet, even as I was making these promises, I was already thinking ahead to Valentine's Day and Easter and all the other opportunities for chocolate.

The diet didn't stand a chance.

One year, I tried resolving to do the kinds of things I already do, and avoid the things I already don't like. I resolved to walk my dog every day, which I had to do because I lived in a condo without a yard. I also promised not to eat foods I disliked or watch movies I hated.

I successfully met my goals that year, but it felt like cheating.

After that, I went back to making resolutions and keeping them with a rather low degree of accuracy. Whether health or career related, they all started strong out of the gate, but didn't have the stamina to cross the finish line in December.

As a matter of fact, I didn't even remember what they were by the end of the year.

This year, I decided to try something different. Maybe the problem with making resolutions on New Year's Day is that I've spent the previous evening at a New Year's Eve party. The lack of sleep alone would be enough to make all promises null and void.

Add champagne and it's a wonder I didn't resolve to stand on my head once a day and get a pet monkey.

So I'm going to wait a week before I sign up to do anything for an entire year. I'll probably set some goals for my health, and for my writing, but I'm also leaning toward a resolution to get to know Placentia better. I've lived here for over thirty years, so you think I'd know a thing or two, but I feel clueless at times.

If nothing else, maybe I can get to one City Council meeting by December.

Today I suddenly wondered whether New Year's resolutions are still made, at least by the younger generation. Maybe the tradition is no longer cool. I asked Marcus if he ever made New Year's resolutions. He nodded, so I asked if he ever kept them.

"Sometimes," he muttered.

I was intrigued. "What kind of resolutions do you make?"

He shrugged. "I don't remember."

I guess the young take their resolutions with as big a grain of salt as their elders do. Or perhaps I shouldn't have tried to talk to him while he was watching TV.

No matter whether we make resolutions or not, another year has scampered by, leaving us to look back and wonder where it all went. Some of us regret the moments wasted, excess food eaten, or useless negativity. Some of us are proud of how much we've accomplished, but still want to do better.

Of course, some people don't review their year at all. Instead, they keep stumbling forward into the next one. They might have a good idea, to not look back.

As Satchel Paige once said, something might be gaining on you.

THE LONG MARCH THROUGH JANUARY

It's January already. When I worked as an engineer, we got the week off (paid) between Christmas and New Year. After the new year, our next holiday was Memorial Day in May, which gave January through April a kind of nose-to-the-grindstone feel.

I can't lie. Going back on that first workday in January felt like the beginning of a long, hard march.

Now that I'm writing, giving riding lessons and volunteering everywhere, my January is a much lighter load. I'd almost enjoy it, if it weren't for the mass chaos that is my house.

My pre-Christmas activities consist of cleaning, decorating, and baking. This year, we hosted Christmas for Dale's family, so the cleaning was a little more intense, and the baking expanded to include actual cooking. Everyone brought a dish, but we were responsible for the turkey (with stuffing), ham, and sweet potatoes.

The week prior, I cleaned at least one room a day. Since Dale's youngest brother and his family live in Lancaster, they were going to spend Christmas night with us. This meant the guest rooms could not serve as clutter stations.

For the first time in months, people were actually going to sleep in them.

Christmas day was fun. We ate, we opened presents, and we ate more. Santa had brought the Carline men exactly what they wanted, which was the return of NBA basketball, so they all sat around and watched the games. I chased everyone out of the kitchen and quietly cleaned up the mess.

On December 26th, my house was still clean.

Now I sit in the family room amid the last shreds of Christmas decorations. Most of the ornaments are on the dining room table, waiting to be boxed. The boxes are in the middle of the living room floor.

I know what must be done. I must gather the decorations, box them, and set them in the hall for Dale to put back in the garage.

The problem is, I noticed our 20-year old cardboard boxes are looking a little weak this year, so I need to go get less destructible plastic bins for the ornaments. I'm not certain how many bins I'll need, or what size. Do I get three large or six smaller ones?

Larger bins have a certain appeal to me. I'm a slave to organization, so I like to sort my decorations into their categories of Tree and Not Tree, and then further into angels, Santas, bells, etc. Smaller boxes mean I find myself making more decisions. Should the angels go with the bells? Does the garland belong with the lights? What about the lighted garland?

Dale might vote for the smaller boxes, since they are a lighter load for him to heft onto the rafters. I probably should do something to make his life easier.

In the meantime, the dishes from two nights ago are calling me from the kitchen. I try to be diligent and keep the dishes washed, but between several parties and Dale's birthday, the dirty pots and pans sank on the priority list, replaced by things like preparing an appetizer to take to the party and getting a present for Dale.

After I finish writing this, I must choose—dishes or decorations? They must both be tackled, but I need one task to stop calling to me while I complete the other. While I'm doing either, I'm sure the rest of the house is piling up dirt, waiting for me to sweep it away.

Excuse me while I take that first step of a very long march. It's January, after all.

RESOLUTIONS, THE SHORT LIST

The problem with writing this column a week in advance is that I have to pretend that I've celebrated the New Year, when in fact I'd like to be in my annual post-Christmas coma. Instead of sleeping all day and resting afterward, I must act as if I've recovered from the holidays and am now back to business as usual.

It's not so bad. I can just write about pretending to make New Year's resolutions.

Each year I make resolutions and each year I either forget about them or realize they were too difficult to keep. Whether I make two resolutions or ten, half of them will be gone by January 3rd.

One resolution I made over Christmas was to use all those limited-time gift cards and coupons I'm given when I purchase gifts for others. I have bought the same gift cards to

163

a popular restaurant for years and gotten my own gift card as a reward each time. The reward expires in March. I've never used it.

That ends in 2013.

A single resolution seems too easy, but I had a hard time thinking of more promises to break. Losing weight and getting healthier are usually part of the list. They're also the first ones tossed, when I'm too busy to sit down to a nice salad and have to eat a drive-thru cheeseburger on my way to the next appointment.

Maybe I could just add a little resolution addendum, where I promise to do better next time.

In desperation this year, I turned to my horoscopes. Horoscopes are those things I don't believe in, unless they happen to be true that day. I also like to believe them when they say something I'd like to be true.

Of course, I also remind myself that they're not written for me, they're written for me and a million other people who share a birth date with me.

My astrological sign is Pisces, the fish. When I looked up my horoscope for 2013, it said my friends and family are going to depend on me so much that I will barely have time for myself. It also said I will meet people who would try to take advantage of me, but my intuition will warn me away from them.

With that kind of prediction, my best resolution is to either go into the witness protection program or adopt a series of disguises for going out in public. And I definitely need to stay away from the phone.

I turned to my Chinese horoscope for better news. As you can imagine, I was born in the Year of the Horse. The Chinese were much kinder to me. According to their prediction, this is a great year for me to gather some wealth. Granted, the amount of wealth was pretty vague, and the source was "from all fronts."

This could either mean my books are going to start selling like hotcakes, a distant relative is going to die and leave me money, or I'm going to start a new career robbing banks.

I'm not sure how to phrase that resolution.

The last part of my horsey horoscope says, "Love is favorable if you are particular. Find someone who wants to take care of you and who will pick up the tab. This is a union that can last."

I'm pretty sure I've got that one covered, although Dale usually treats me as though I can take care of myself.

So I'm left with a pretty short list of resolutions this year. I just need to strengthen my resolve—or pretend better.

MAKING A NEW YEAR'S LIST AND CHECKING IT TWICE

Happy New Year! Have you made, attempted, and abandoned your resolutions yet?

The word resolution has a few meanings. The one we attach with the new year is "a decision or determination; a resolve." Each January, we resolve to do things better or change our lives in some way.

By February, we've resolved that most of those decisions weren't feasible, but at least we tried.

The other meaning for resolution is "a formal expression of intention made, usually after voting, by a formal organization." Can you imagine what our New Year's resolutions would look like if they were made by a committee?

Having served on a few committees, I'm sure they'd

have to start in February to even have a viable list of resolutions by the end of December. First, they'd have to decide how many resolutions to make. Is one too few? Are ten too many?

The debate on that would last until June, assuming they meet once a month.

Actually, I suppose the first order of business would be to determine when and where to meet. I'm currently on a committee that will be presiding over a large event at the end of March. We need to meet and get things organized, but no one can pick a common time to get together.

I'm pretty sure what one of the "lessons learned" items will be afterward.

Having a group of people choose what you should change about your life might be interesting. If I use my life as an example, what would others want to change about me?

Some people might want me to take things more seriously, although some might prefer my carefree attitude. Others might want me to present a more polished exterior, while another contingent thinks my jeans-and-t-shirt wardrobe suits me. And then there is the eating and exercise delegation, who think I should do less of one and more of the other.

With enough people debating, these items could remain in deadlock all summer.

Even if the committee goes smoothly and submits its final list, would you use it? I realize that there are some people who enjoy taking advice from others and would welcome any tips for making their lives better. On the flip side, it might infuriate some people to be told what to do.

I'm probably in the middle of those two extremes. As an author, I've gotten used to critiques of my work, and even negative reviews. Instead of getting defensive, I consider the remark and often change what I've written because I think they're right.

As a person making day-to-day choices, I've often joked, the day someone wants to pay my bills, they can tell me how to live my life. And I've been in situations where people are yelling orders at me. My reaction is always to do the complete opposite of what they're screaming.

So, as long as the list is entitled "Recommendations for New Year's Resolutions" and it's not shrieking at me in capital letters, I might use it.

Perhaps it's better if we resolve to make our own decisions. Even if our loved ones can see us more clearly from the outside than we can from the inside, we are ultimately the ones responsible for our own lives.

I might ask for suggestions, but I think I'll make my own list.

RESOLVING TO BE KIND TO OTHERS, AND MYSELF

Wait, is it almost 2015 already? Where did our year go? At my age, I may have just misplaced it and will find it in the junk drawer when I finally clean that out.

The ending of one year and beginning of another means it is time for us to take stock of what we did well and what we could improve. We make another list of resolutions. Some of them we even keep, if you define "keep" as "writing it down in a notebook and never looking at it again."

Every year I think that New Year's resolutions are stupid and everyone over-promises and under-delivers and we should stop making them. Then I find a notepad and start writing.

As 2014 has progressed, I've been obsessed with kindness and what that means. One of the things that struck me about traveling in Scotland was their attention to being

169

nice to one another. They even had signs on the road encouraging people to be calm and let faster drivers pass, in order to avoid accidents.

I wonder if signs like that could cure our tendencies toward road rage.

In particular, I loved their displays about Scottish independence. We were there a month before the vote, and everywhere we went, there were large, blue "YES" signs. Underneath many of them, we saw smaller, purple signs that said, "No, Thanks."

How polite is that? I wish our elections were that nice.

This year's resolutions, for me, are going to revolve around kindness. I'm resolving to be kinder to people. I'm not exactly a Grinch, so I'm hoping this isn't harder than it sounds.

It's easy for me to let someone go ahead of me in line, or to keep a bag of plastic bottles to give to the man in the wheelchair in the parking lot, or to pick up a box in the aisle and put it back on the shelf.

Where kindness gets harder is when I'm trying to override the initial anger of being cut off in traffic, or watching the person ahead of me knock something over, look at it, and keep walking. Are these people being self-absorbed? Maybe. Is my irritation justified? Possibly.

But my day would be brighter and my blood pressure would be lower if I could smile and shrug and find something kind to think about them instead.

I know this won't be easy, so my kindness resolution is going to extend to myself as well. First, since the New Year involves a review of the past, I'm going to stop and congratulate myself on what I managed to get done. And I'm going to resolve that, if I have a moment of meanness in 2015,

I'm going to apologize, promise to do better, and keep going.

So many of our resolutions, once broken, are abandoned. Why do we do that? If there's something we want to improve, the last thing on our list should be, "I resolve to keep working on this list until I make a new one for next year."

Whatever you resolve for the New Year, I hope you take a moment to pat yourself on the back for what you've done so far. Go ahead and resolve to be a better person, but give yourself permission to get there in baby steps.

We're all in this together.

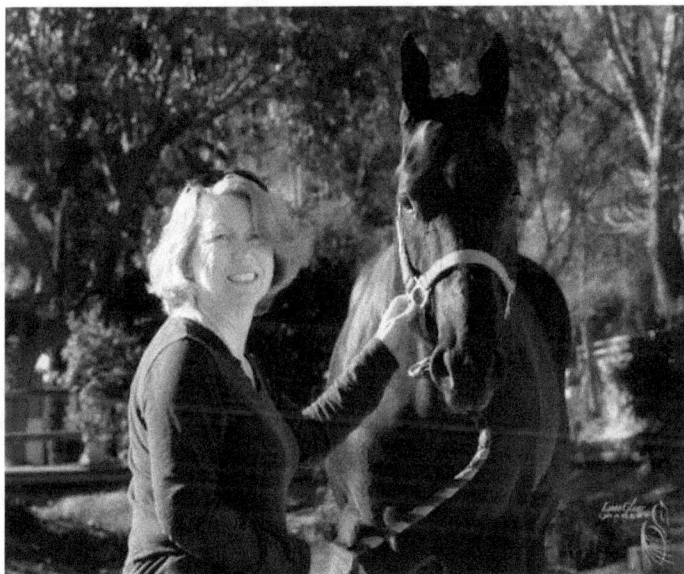

ABOUT THE AUTHOR

Gayle Carline is a typical Californian, meaning she was born somewhere else. She moved to Orange County from Illinois in 1978, and landed in Placentia a few years later.

Her husband, Dale, bought her a laptop for Christmas in 1999 because she wanted to write. A year after that, he gave her horseback riding lessons. When she bought her first horse, she finally started writing.

Gayle soon became a regular contributor to California Riding Magazine, and in March, 2005, she began writing a humor column for her local newspaper, the Placentia News-Times. Every week, she entertains readers with stories of her life with Dale and their son, Marcus.

Believing she should experience reincarnation while she is still alive, Gayle has been a software engineer, a dancer, and even a flying angel for the Crystal Cathedral's Glory of Christmas.

In her spare time, Gayle likes to sit down with friends and laugh over a glass of wine. Or two.

For more merriment, visit her at http://www.gaylecarline.com.

ALSO BY THIS AUTHOR

Freezer Burn (A Peri Minneopa Mystery)
Hit or Missus (A Peri Minneopa Mystery)
The Hot Mess (A Peri Minneopa Mystery)
Clean Sweep (A Peri Minneopa Short Story)

Murder on the Hoof

From the Horse's Mouth: One Lucky Memoir

What Would Erma Do? Confessions of a First Time
Humor Columnist
Are You There, Erma? It's Me Gayle
Raising the Perfect Family and Other Tall Tales
You're from Where?

GAYLE CARLINE

www.ingramcontent.com/pod-product-compliance
Lightning Source LLC
LaVergne TN
LVHW051404080426
835508LV00022B/2967